TEN GOING ON TWELVE

TEN GOING ON TWELVE

Claire Tétreau Brandt
and
Patricia McCune Irvine

iUniverse, Inc.
New York Lincoln Shanghai

Ten Going On Twelve

iUniverse books may be ordered through booksellers or by contacting:

iUniverse
2021 Pine Lake Road, Suite 100
Lincoln, NE 68512
www.iuniverse.com
1-800-Authors (1-800-288-4677)

ISBN-13: 978-0-595-40958-7 (pbk)
ISBN-13: 978-0-595-85317-5 (ebk)
ISBN-10: 0-595-40958-X (pbk)
ISBN-10: 0-595-85317-X (ebk)

Printed in the United States of America

A la mémoire de
Maman et Papa
avec beaucoup d'amour

CHAPTER 1

On that special morning in Sanford, Maine, back in 1921, a mid-winter blizzard hurled snow against the windows of the two-story home on State Street. The wind rattled the old doors and freezing air swirled through cracks to mingle with the cozy inside. A black iron stove warmed the room, and a reservoir on the side heated water needed for the home birth, imminent now.

The children had been dispatched to relatives. The little boys, Joseph Egide Paul (called Paul) and Joseph Henri (called Henri) were taken in by *Tante* Agathe. With her brood, what were two more? Laurette and Marguerite were pleased to go with *Tante* Souzanne for a couple of days. All were happy with their cousins.

Maman's sister, Virgenie, and other relatives, were there to help with the ordeal that was sure to come. Nine siblings hoped for another brother. But a sister would be all right. Each new baby was another playmate. And the newest, tiniest one was always Papa's pet, Papa who ate supper many evenings with a baby on his lap. He loved his family and each child knew she, or he, was Papa's most favorite.

Already seven pretty girls and two lively little boys were part of the Tétreau family. And joy and amusement needed no outside assistance.

And so, with the blizzard howling outdoors, Aurelie Tétreau's new baby was born. Number Ten. Another girl. Me. And as the boys' first names were always Joseph, the girls' first names were always Marie. I was Marie Claire Therese (called Claire). My papa's new favorite.

For two days, the snow fell and piled on the already white ground. Maples and elms bent over, heavy with new snow, the wind dangerously strong. My siblings were happy to stay a few more days with the cousins. Moving about was not possible in that winter storm.

What a start in life.

*   *   *   *

Papa—Alfred Tétreau—was our guiding light. In our small town, he had a tailoring business, a busy shop on the second floor of a building on Main Street, where he designed and tailored suits and altered fur coats.

Papa also had a dry-cleaning business, and the equipment, a huge drum about six feet in height, with a door for loading clothes, was in a small house in our big yard on State Street. The siblings often played in that little house and Papa always warned, "*Arrêtez-vous là.*" Stand back, before he added gasoline or kerosene and turned on the drum to gyrate and clean the clothes.

I always liked the smell of gasoline, probably because it was part of Papa's work, and even today when we fill the gas tank of our car, memories of those dry-cleaning days return. Every time.

*   *   *   *

Because the father of so many little ones needed transportation that was not only safe, but could be used in his work, Papa designed a small white house to fasten on his truck. The words, TÉTREAU THE TAILOR, were emblazoned on the four-sided roof. I, personally, like to believe it was one of the first campers in the state of Maine. Not only was Papa's work advertised as he drove, but lots of room was provided for the children on family outings to one of the many ponds—Long Pond in the town of Shapleigh was my favorite—or Wells Beach, twelve miles down the road to the Atlantic ocean. I remember the narrow benches on the sides of the truck bed made especially for us.

"Sit here," Papa said. "Paul, Henri. Come on, girls, you, too. Rose. Delia." They did as he said and crowded together on the benches, all of them, some on each side, while I sat on *Maman's* lap, in the front with Papa.

Papa was credited with another innovation: he placed signs in a row on the roadsides of our town to promote his tailor shop. Many years later, I often saw the well-known Burma Shave ads along the highways. Too bad, Burma Shave—I think my papa was there first.

Papa did other things. So many shoes to buy. So many little teeth for Dr. Miller, the dentist, to take care of.

Well, Papa made arrangements with the shoe store owner: "When my children need shoes, just handle it," Papa said to the shoe man. "I will pay."

But Papa wasn't happy when Victorine bought size four shoes when she should have ordered size six, and her toes were squeezed way beyond the comfort zone.

Even so, Papa made a similar arrangement for payment with the dentist. "Just take care of all the teeth," Papa said. And Dr. Miller did.

And Victorine didn't mess with that.

Dear Victorine. Number Five. Always the prankster, the instigator, the tease, who had to sit next to *Maman* at the supper table so *Maman* could keep her in line.

We were raised in a home where all sat down to dinner together, to share good conversation as well as to eat. But no acting up was allowed.

This rule was difficult for Victorine, our comic. On more than one night, she sat stony-faced, but somehow, so innocently, so secretly, entertained her sisters. She blinked and twitched and rolled her eyes. We struggled not to laugh. But first one of us was sent from the table, then another, until Victorine was almost the only girl left, before Papa figured out her prank and called us back.

"No acting up at the table, Vickie," Papa scolded, but his dark eyes were soft and his voice tender. Because he was a jokester himself.

And he also knew very well Victorine was the one who could change a somber gathering into a lively group in almost no time at all.

What would our large household have done without Papa? Our dear papa.

✳   ✳   ✳   ✳

Behind the barn was a vintage coach, a shiny black horse-drawn carriage. Exquisite bevel-edged glass decorated the sides and back of the vehicle. An ornate gas lamp guarded each door.

Papa had been a mortician many years before, but gave it up for his family's security when an epidemic of diphtheria was widespread. His fabulous carriage became a playhouse for all the sisters.

I vividly remember a gift to me of a doll, with her suitcase brim full of little clothes. How many hours I spent changing my doll's dresses in that playhouse! Even the boys, Paul and Henri, visited, if only to cause upheaval in the girls' playroom.

And never once, in all the years, did I think of that enchanted castle as a one-time carriage for departing souls on their way to heaven.

✳   ✳   ✳   ✳

I can't remember the time I didn't adore my whole family. We spoke French. We bunched together in all the beds to sleep. And went to Mass. My life was filled with small town values. As I looked around I saw Aurelie, *la belle Maman,* surrounded by a cluster of pretty daughters, plus two handsome sons. This was my family. From Number One, Antoinette, to Number Ten, thirteen years later. Me. Claire.

Would I ever remember all their names?

Mais certainment. I did learn all the names. From the very beginning. Without the slightest trouble.

We had such a great family. Could it be real? So much affection? Such good times?

Or was it I who was in a cloud? Were we really not our own selves, Antoinette, Bertha, Rose, and all the others? Were we all just Pollyannas, truly? Does my memory flicker because it is now 2005 and some of us, most of us, are gone?

Have I begun to paint the pictures with a new brush, to cover the cracks and rough spots, so only the goodness shows, the sparkle, the sweetness?

No. I don't think so.

Everything is there, mixed together—the tough times, the joys. And sadness, too. But we played the game of life together; we cared about one another. And created a stirring pathway through the years. Anyway, that's how I look back on it.

And one good thing: I was never lonely.

But one not so good thing: I never really made a decision on my very own. Worse, I never really even thought about making one. No necessity. And sometimes, as the years passed, now and then, when I had to, I made some decisions that were, as it turned out, inferior. Inadequate. On occasion, even worse than that.

CHAPTER 2

▼

Through the years, I rarely thought of anything beyond life with my special *Maman* and dear papa, my sisters and two big brothers, my aunts and uncles and dozens of cousins.

Now, I find I'm strangely comforted to remember some history about my little town of Sanford, and its counterpart, the village of Springvale, in York County, Maine, located at the base of Mount Hope in the White Mountains. And to recall some of the town's prelude and metamorphoses as the years raced by.

Of course, today, Sanford is a busy industrial town of more than twenty thousand inhabitants. Stream-lined restaurants and department stores in shopping centers have replaced the small family-owned businesses on Main Street, the shoe store, the hardware store, Tétreau the friendly tailor.

But in the early, early days of our sprawling new country, Sanford began along the Saco River with twelve sawmills, and almost no people. The land was called Phillipstown, simply because a lumberman named William Phillips bought the large area from a couple of local Indian chiefs.

"It was best to buy the land from the Indians," I said to *Maman* more than a few hundred years later, "buying it is not so awful as taking it away from them by force. Or killing them for it."

But *Maman* really had no time to think about Phillipstown. Or Sanford, either. Any more than I did then. And certainly Papa was much too busy.

Anyway, time dashed by as usual, and in ninety years or so, when Mr. Phillips was no longer around, an unofficial census listed one hundred residents.

Farmers and woodsmen continued to trickle in, population increased, and by 1768 town status was finally reached. At that time, Maine was actually a province of Massachusetts, so the Governor of Massachusetts signed the incorporation papers. He also decided to change the name—which was his right—to Sanford, in honor of Peleg Sanford, one-time Governor of Rhode Island and stepson of William Phillips.

Just about everyone farmed until the late 1860's when Thomas Goodall established The Goodall Mills. And then just about everyone worked in the mills. Sanford became a mill town and skilled workers from French-speaking provinces of Canada arrived along with those from other foreign countries.

Many years later, when Aurelie and Alfred Tétreau were raising their family, the Goodall Mills introduced the Palm Beach label for producing clothing material, to add to their commercial products of blankets and carriage robes and auto fabrics and uniforms and railroad car upholstery.

Several of the Tétreau girls, and everyone else in town, began to work in the mills as soon as they graduated from high school. Well, almost everyone. Antoinette worked for Dr. Cobb and Dr. Ross. Papa, of course, had his own business.

I always thought the day would come when I, too, would work in the mills. But that never happened.

And every once in awhile, I wondered if those early, skilled, French-speaking mill workers from provinces of Canada were actually my ancestors. Of course, when I grew up in Sanford, I rarely thought about my ancestors. I was concerned only for the moment. And I believed everyone in the world spoke French. Or probably should.

But on one of the many walks *Maman* and I had together, around the neighborhood, she told me she herself was born in Canada.

"In Ste. Agathe-des-Monts, Québec," she said, a hint of pride in her clear voice. "I was a Langlois."

"What about Papa? Where was Papa born?"

"Your papa was born in Vermont. Rutland, Vermont. And he came to Sanford as a little boy. I was already here. Aren't you glad?" She smiled at me, a bit mischievously, I think now, as my mind slips back.

Sanford had no trains in those early days. No busses. Not even the vaguest thought of an airport.

But the Goodall Mansion, built in 1871, still stands amid clusters of pines and maples and elms in the center of town. And the not-so-old Goodall Hospital on June Street is still meeting health care needs of the community. Sanford has a Goodall Memorial Library and a Goodall Park.

Rivers flowed through town. The Mousam River was the main one and the Mousam Falls provided waterpower for the early mills. And by 1925, nearly all the old wooden buildings had been replaced by new structures of brick, steel and concrete.

To the west of town, the terrain was hilly as it slipped unevenly down from the mountain, and shaded with elm trees and maples and conifers, dotted with ponds and lakes. A bit of heaven in summer.

In winter, our ponds and rivers froze and ice and snow whirled and swirled about us and prepared the hills for exciting sledding.

I loved to romp in the cold on those frigid snowy days, to ride in Bertha's protective arms on her sled down the slippery slopes.

And sometimes, I romanticize about the source of my strange tolerance to extreme cold and pain. Could it be the heart and soul, the quintessence, of the monumental blizzard that accompanied my birth?

And on many steamy summer days, we all piled in the back of Papa's truck and were off on our family outings to one of the ponds or to Wells Beach. Those days were not the time to wonder about ancestors or history or the mills. Those were the fun, family times, with the togetherness and bliss of childhood.

*   *   *   *

Early one April morning, much to my surprise, I learned a new baby had arrived at our house, secretly, in the night. Another girl, of course. Adrienne. A tiny little one.

The entire household was aflutter, but Bertha was the most thrilled of all. Because that very day was her own birthday, too.

"Elle est à moi—un cadeau spécial," Bertha squealed so everyone could hear and would know the truth. She's my special present. She's my special present. She's mine. She really is.

*   *   *   *

Although every Tétreau secretly prayed for another boy whenever *Maman* gave birth, after Henri, those prayers were never answered.

So everyone was relieved the brothers were close enough in age to be pals, to make a special twosome. Paul and Henri.

Paul, Number Eight, the first-born son, took his status of heir-apparent seriously. He had Papa's black hair and was always praised for having the most striking black eyes. At least the rest of us considered it praise. But not Paul.

"Cheri, que saites-tu?" Maman asked one day when she found him washing his eyes with soap. What are you doing?

He jerked his head up and squinted through the lather. "Everyone talks about my black eyes, and I'm just trying to wash the dirt out, so they will be clean like everyone else's. That's what I'm trying to do. Only it isn't working."

"Oh, *bébé.*"

Paul, with the gorgeous eyes.

Being the first boy in an array of seven pretty and popular girls was not an easy life for him. He became doubly masculine and courageous, not only to secure his position in the world, but so no one would dare call him a sissy. And no one ever did. He actually became a war hero, all five feet six inches, one hundred thirty pounds of him, a Fighting Marine. But that was much later, in World War II.

Now brother, Henri, Number Nine, was a dear, sweet, genuine gem. He never refused a cry for help nor request for a favor from anyone, any time. Even to teaching his baby sister, me, to dance, a favorite pastime of all of us—later, though, when the time was right.

Even though Adrienne was always special to Bertha because they shared the same birthday, Adrienne and I created another family twosome as we grew older. No one was surprised. We became inseparable. But not quite like Paul and Henri, who were the only boys, smothered by sisters on all sides.

And not really like Laurette and Marguerite, either, who were so close in age they were in the same class at school.

I particularly remember Marguerite was the more studious of those two and was often chastised for failing to get Laurette's homework done on time.

Someone always reminded her: "Marguerite, *qu'as-tu? Pourquoi vas-tu lentement? L'ecole commençe. Dépêche-toi. Laurette est prête.*" What's the matter with you? Why are you so slow? It's time for school. Hurry. Laurette's ready to go.

Poor Marguerite.

Nor were Adrienne and I a twosome like Rose and Delia, who were the tallest sisters, athletic, who played tennis together through the years and were always each other's best friend.

Precious Rose was the beauty with long blond tresses and dazzling blue eyes, and Delia, who smiled the best of all of us, was the one who helped *Maman* the most, and sewed clothes for the whole bunch. Delia became an excellent seamstress at a very young age.

No. Adrienne and I had our own special twosome. Not like any other.

And in time, when she was old enough, I would say, "*Voilà,* Adrienne, *le wagon-fruit sonne. Allons chercher la glace.*"

And together we ran to the fruit man, who was also the iceman. He had bushels of McIntosh apples. And pears by the peck. Grapes. Great bunches of bananas to hang and ripen in the barn. And huge slabs of ice for the neighborhood ice boxes.

While housewives checked out the fruit, kids milled around to watch the iceman chip the ice to the proper sizes. He never failed to give each of us a good chunk to hold with freezing fingers and to suck with a frigid mouth that sometimes made our teeth ache. But that ice was so good. Even now, thinking about it.

Merci, Mr. Iceman, thank you.

CHAPTER 3

▼

While Adrienne was still too little, I tagged after the older sisters. Especially when the snow was deep and they headed, with their sleds, for the closest hill.

One particular winter day, when the snow was soft and luscious-looking, the sky clear and a hard bright blue, Laurette and Marguerite each with a new sled, took off together for a nearby snow-covered hill. They paid no attention to four-year old me who, with a large, ancient sled, dragged myself behind them.

By the time I reached the top of the slope, they both were on their way down, and whizzed like the wind on their new sleds.

I quickly hopped on mine, gave a shove with my feet, and raced as close behind them as I could.

What a thrill. Never before had I been on a sled by myself.

Once in flight, I was electrified. Snow flew in my face. I held my breath. My hands clenched the sides of the sled.

But the ecstasy lasted only seconds. Because I was not in control of the big sled. At first, I was surprised, then stunned. When sudden panic took charge, I screamed.

"Laurette! *Secours!* Help! I can't stop. I'm going too fast. Marguerite!"

Then I crashed. Smack into a fence of pointy barbed wire.

I bellowed for a moment. And then was silent.

My sisters came quickly.

Marguerite took one look, and her eyes blinked a few times. "You'd better go home," she said.

"Yes," Laurette agreed. "You'd better go home right now. This minute."

They picked me up and sent me on my way.

I sloshed back through the snow alone, dragged my heavy sled behind me, and bawled all the way to our house.

Maman heard me and rushed out, gathered me to her, and carried me inside.

"*Bébé, bébé.*" she soothed, "Where do you hurt?"

"Everywhere, *Maman*."

The problem was not visible until my snowsuit was removed. Then all was clear—a gash, almost to the bone, across the front of my right thigh. Flesh had separated and the wound bled profusely. The barbed wire had penetrated the snowsuit to tear my leg, but had not torn the wool. Strange.

Maman called and both Dr. Cobb and Dr. Ross rushed to the house. Twenty-six stitches were needed to close the wound— the ugly scar is still with me—twenty-six stitches on a four-year-old's thigh is a lot of stitches.

Enough to keep me, for the rest of the winter, propped up for hours at the window, in a padded turned-upside-down kitchen chair, where my leg was protected and more comfortable. And as my wound healed itself, I watched the crowd skate at the rink

Papa had built next door, to keep his teen-age girls at home—away from all the eager boys in town.

I didn't reflect much on the event until years later, when I wondered how my busy parents could keep track of so many children and I questioned whether my accident might have been avoided.

And did Papa's skating rink keep the older girls at home? Away from the town boys? Because everybody in Sanford knew Aurelie and Alfred Tétreau always kept a firm, loving hand on their ever-growing flock.

What I concluded is maybe true and maybe not. But I decided *Maman* and Papa took care of the important issues: the morals, work ethics, responsibilities, loyalty, sharing, watching over each other. And allowed the little things to take care of themselves.

And most of the time, the older kids in the Tétreau family watched over the younger ones. Even if I did crash my heavy old sled into the barbed wire fence when I was four years old. And trudged home by myself, dragging my sled behind me.

And about the skating rink: when Rose and Delia asked for permission to skate on Sanford's frozen Mousam River, Papa shook his head. "All the boys in town meet there," he said. "I'll make a rink for you here, where you'll be safe."

And the very next morning, in our spacious side yard, Papa made a frame of wood for a skating rink. He filled it with water and hosed it down every night.

Voilà, a skating rink.

This was not what his pretty teen-age daughters hoped for, but it soon became a gathering place for skaters, especially the boys from all over town.

And everyone had a wonderful time, except me—because I could only watch from the window.

✳   ✳   ✳   ✳

I pondered a bit that winter as I sat in the padded turned-upside-down kitchen chair and gazed out the window at the world. I learned to think about 'things.'

I'd always been self-confident. I knew everyone loved me. As I loved everyone. I was Papa's favorite, of course. I was as pretty as my sisters with my black hair and hazel eyes. Papa said so. And I'd be five years old in a few weeks.

Just why was I inside watching all the fun happening outside on Papa's rink? I was so restless, so anxious to be out there with everyone.

My mind continued to agitate. Why was I so inept that I'd run my sled into the barbed wire fence?

"Maman! I want to go outside!"

But *Maman* had already begun the morning ritual of baking bread. So many loaves. At least twelve. Some were already baked and stacked about the kitchen. The aroma that permeated the entire house was heavenly.

I watched *Maman's* capable hands knead the dough and form the loaves and in turn place them in the oven. I had her entirely to myself those days, and whether or not I understood her lessons, I listened as she shared her many deep thoughts.

"Always go to Mass," she said more than once, "and when it's time, be sure to marry a nice Catholic boy. Make certain he's French. Be honest. Pay your debts."

Sometimes *Maman* sang a song with me. Sheer joy. But my restless and anxious and childish mind also missed the companionship of the skaters.

"Maman. I want to go outside."

My mind kept its circuitous and worthless route.

"Maman—"

Surely, life wasn't meant to be spent propped up on a chair, watching others through a window.

My thoughts spun all the way around to a few nights earlier when I'd reached out my hand with a glass to help *Maman* set the table. After I placed the glass—well, it wasn't on the table at all. No. It lay in a million pieces on the floor. I suppose that wasn't so terrifying to me as running my old sled into the barbed wire fence, but a scary mystery, anyway. I said I was sorry. More than once.

"I'm sorry, *Maman.* I'm sorry. I didn't mean to break the glass."

Maman was so busy in the kitchen then, cooking dinner for all of us, she just looked at me and smiled as if to say, "Never mind, *bébé.* It's all right."

Rose, always ready when help was needed, found a broom and swept the shards into a dustpan and carried it away.

But why was I so awkward? Why couldn't I put a glass on the table without dropping it on the floor? Worrisome questions like that tumbled out of my head without my having any say-so in the matter. I knew my secret was deeper than being clumsy. Darker. More secretive. Scarier. Something I didn't understand. I closed my mind and stared out the window. I didn't want to think about any more 'things.'

Well, while I was at it, just one more 'thing.'

Why didn't I have a long beautiful name that flowed over everyone's tongues, like An-toi-nette and Mar-guer-ite and Vic-to-rine and Del-i-a and A-dri-enne?

Claire had only one very plain sound to it. Even the other girls had at least two sounds. Like Ber-tha or Lau-rette.

Only Rose and I had one-sound names and Rose was a perfect name for her because she was so precious herself. Besides she had a touch of natural wave in her blond hair that folded neatly across her head, much like petals on a real rose.

But a one-sound name like Claire? I didn't like it at all. Not one little bit.

Now, from where I am today, writing this, I'm sure I thought a lot about those 'things,' but I believe not while I sat at the window in the turned-upside-down padded chair that winter. I believe all I needed at that time was a cozy atmosphere, the delicious aroma of *Maman's* baking bread and the security and reassuring sight of happy people. I don't know, of course, but I suspect all the serious thinking came later, when I was older. When 'things' were different.

CHAPTER 4

▼

The early morning was gray. The house was cold. No chance to run to the warm, black, cast iron kitchen stove, open the oven door and put my feet as close to the hot air as I dared. No, none of that.

Because no one had started the fire in the stove.

Where was *Maman*? I didn't know. But the house was full of people. My older sisters hunched together on the stairs. Crying about something. Aunts and uncles made their way around them and up and down the staircase and through all the rooms. I didn't see my brothers at all. Voices were hushed. Strange men came and left.

Then all was quiet and dark.

The next day was exactly the same. Dismal and scary and cold. Only a large box was in the living room. I stood very still. Where was my papa? I'd better wake my papa. I moved toward the box. Someone stopped me.

"No, Claire. Your papa is—"

"He's just sleeping. I can wake him. I know I can. He's just sleeping."

"No, Claire."

And I was pulled away.

Papa was only forty-four years old when he died. And I was five. And *Maman* was eight months pregnant. I didn't know it then, but she was.

"A heart attack," I heard from one of the visitors.

"He was fine the other night," from another. "We played our weekly card game here. He was just like always. Lots of fun. Joking. Eating. Drinking a little home brew. Not too much. I can't believe—"

No one could believe. But it was true. Our wonderful papa was gone.

I squeezed my eyes shut and my face grew tight. Oh, my Papa. I held my breath without being aware. And tried to understand.

But it was true.

My dear papa had gone to heaven.

*   *   *   *

Of course, I didn't understand *Maman's* position during those first, dark, traumatic days. In the years since, I have thought of her a lot. She was so brave. So stalwart. And not once did any of us see her cry. Not once.

Eleven children to take care of, and another expected any moment. *Maman* was the family cook and seamstress, the house manager. And now must persevere alone. Without the loving assistance of her dear mate.

When Papa's business and lodge friends offered to sponsor some of the children, to take them and care for them in their own homes, with their own families, *Maman* refused.

"We want to help you," they said. "We need to help you."

But *Maman* would have no outside restrictions on the raising of her brood. If she had to adjust alone, with the pain and pressure of the great world on her shoulders, that's what she would do.

"*Non,*" she said emphatically, "*Je suis très contente de votre gentilesse, mais je ne peux séparer même pas un de mes enfants de la famille! Je vous remercie. Mais tous ensemble, il peut nous débrouiller. Grâce à Dieu.*"

She appreciated their kindness, but told them she could not separate even one of her babies from the rest of the family. They must all stay together. She thanked the kind men, but the family would manage. With God's help.

What a great and respected woman Aurelie Tétreau was.

Because now, new baby coming or not, Aurelie realized her only course of action, her only source of income, was to keep Papa's tailor and dry cleaning shop open.

She, a master seamstress, became the tailor. Rose and Delia took over the task of dry cleaning and pressing the clothes, an arduous task for two immature teens still in school.

Bertha, the cautious one, the new stabilizer of the family, and most beloved, took over the role of mother, to fix the scraped knees and dry the sad tears for the rest of us while *Maman* was at the Tailor Shop.

Antoinette, however, had graduated from high school and this was the point in time and the reason Dr. Cobb and Dr. Ross offered her a job.

"We'll train her to be a helper," Dr. Ross said to *Maman*. "It's one way we can assist you and your family. We truly want to do this."

"Merci," Maman said, *"Merci beaucoup."*

"Thanks," Antoinette, the unskilled teen, added.

She started to work for the doctors the next day.

*   *   *   *

Louise, a lovely little blonde princess, was born early. So I was told. Number Twelve. The last. Another girl and a joy to everyone.

Nevertheless, a new difficult uneasiness hovered about *Maman* that was never apparent when Papa was our leader and our strength.

*   *   *   *

One sunny day, a month or so later, I accompanied *Maman* to the corner grocery store for flour and milk. I carried a clean, empty quart bottle for Mr. Guillemette to fill from one of his five gallon milk containers.

I skipped and jumped along the way as I always did. I ran and twirled and played a kind of hopscotch—

> Don't step on a crack,
> You'll break your mother's back.

"Where have you been?" Mr. Guillemette asked *Maman*. "You've stopped coming here. Where have you gone for your groceries? I know you're not charging anything, anywhere, these days, Mrs. Tétreau, but I insist you charge your purchases here again. Like you always have."

"But Mr. Guillemette—"

"No. I insist. I know you will not abuse the privilege. I know you will pay me some day."

And I, for one, as young as I was, knew the flour, eggs and milk made the best *crêpes. Maman* was such a superb *crêpe* maker. And the aroma of fresh homemade bread, when someone is baking nearby, brings a nostalgia that overcomes me even now, these many years later,

*   *   *   *

And so the weeks slipped away.

Before I knew it, I was ready for my first day of school. The September morning was still warm with summer and I wished we were on a family outing to Sand Pond or Picture Pond or Old Fishing Pond instead of dragging off to school.

We were still in mourning for Papa so I wore my black pleated dress with the wide belt, black stockings and black shoes. I had a Dutch boy haircut, except my hair was black instead of yellow.

I was scared to death.

We hurried across the back yard, up the hilly path to the top, sneaked around houses and took a short cut through the alley to Main Street and the school.

I trailed behind Bertha and Rose and Delia and all the others—except the two brothers who ran on ahead, and Antoinette who had already graduated and was working for Dr. Cobb and Dr. Ross. I wished one of the others would take my hand. But no one did.

The church-school, St. Ignatius, was a large brick building. Two graceful stairways adorned the front hall that opened to the classrooms.

"No, we don't go in that way," Victorine said when I moved toward the door.

"Except on very special occasions," Bertha explained, with such kindness in her voice I wanted to run to her, or maybe even cry.

But I did neither, and we continued around to the stairs in the back, where other pupils gathered.

"There's your classroom, Claire," Bertha said, the same sweetness in her voice, as if she knew I was almost paralyzed with dread. Then she steered me in the right direction and gave me a little nudge.

"I don't want to go in there," I said, but in such a low whisper no one heard me. In a moment my siblings were out of sight and I was alone.

The Sister didn't appear to be surprised another Tétreau had started school, but I was lost in a horror that washed over me in waves. My stomach fluttered, but my brain closed down. I wished desperately to be at the Tailor Shop with *Maman* and Adrienne and *Bébé* Louise.

That first day of school was the beginning of a misery that stuck to me through all my school years. School was forever a nightmare.

And as if that first black school day was not already full of sufficient terror, more of it surfaced when I found myself locked in the little girls' room alone after school was out. I couldn't help it. I had to go. And how was the old janitor supposed to know I was still in there when he locked up for the day?

I banged on the door and called out through my tight throat, but the room was under the school and on the side of the church, and no one knew I was there, a dark, dank scary, lonely cellar to me. I pounded on the door until my fists were sore. I bawled out for help in tones as loud as I could muster.

"*Secours! Secours! Venez! Vite!*" Help. Help. Please. Somebody help. Hurry.

Finally, after ages, I heard the key in the lock. I was rescued. At last. *I was rescued.*

As soon as I was free, I bolted. And called, *"Merci, merci,"* over my shoulder. The janitor didn't even have a chance to scold me.

But I couldn't go home.

I didn't remember the way.

I had to wait until someone in my family noticed I was missing and returned to get me. I plopped down on the bottom step and squeezed my eyes shut. Warm tears slowly rolled down my cheeks and splashed delicately on the ground and on my shoes and on the cement steps.

CHAPTER 5

▼

Every morning we headed for school early enough to attend Mass and then off to the Tailor Shop for breakfast. There, on a potbellied stove, *Maman* had a big pan of oatmeal cooking, with brown sugar and cinnamon.

I still love that meal. Sometimes, I wonder if it's because of memories of the sweet aroma and taste, or thoughts of *Maman's* being ready with our breakfast at the shop every morning, in spite of all her never-ending chores.

Often, we returned after school. I sometimes stood at the big second-story window and watched the people outside and noted expressions on their faces. The smiles, or frowns, the laughter. Sometimes anger. Worry. People in a rush or idling slowly.

One lady, a cigarette hanging from her mouth, held a baby in one arm and a bag of groceries in the other. Not a pleasant picture with that dangling cigarette. But I learned something: beware of your demeanor, I told myself. Someone out there may be watching you. And from then on, I tried to make certain my lips were relaxed in a smile. I still have the habit—smile, Claire, someone may be watching you.

We all knew the third floor of the building was filled with equipment, dishes and pots and pans left over from an old restaurant.

So, one afternoon, Adrienne, who always had good ideas, said to me with a sparkle in her eyes, "Claire, let's go upstairs and look around."

That sounded like a marvelous idea to me and we raced up the stairs as fast as we could.

We started to move dishes and pots and pans around and then Adrienne held up a bottle of vinegar and called out, "Look! Look at all the vinegar bottles! There must be a hundred here. I wonder why the restaurant owner needed so much vinegar."

I'd found something by then. "How about this?" I showed her a box of baking soda. "There must be a hundred of these soda boxes, too."

"Well, watch me," Adrienne said.

In a rapid, rhythmic movement, she grabbed a china cup, poured vinegar in it and added baking soda. And together we watched the sparkling effervescence. We filled another cup with vinegar and added soda and watched it foam and gurgle and bubble and fizz. And another cup. And another. For a long time.

We made a monumental mess. And left it there.

Usually, Rose and Delia checked on us if we were too quiet, but on that wonderful day of discovery, they were much too busy pressing clothes in the shop downstairs.

I didn't give it a thought then, but when I was older I realized the big sisters had all the problems, the worries, and did all the work to help *Maman*. They baby-sat while the three littlest sisters had all the fun and made all the messes.

✳   ✳   ✳   ✳

Apples were ripening on the trees. McIntosh. My favorites, even now. Back then, on our way to and from school, we watched and waited. Many modest homes on the tree-lined streets had McIntosh apples in the yards.

"Those apples will be ripe enough to pick pretty soon," Victorine said, with a sharpness in her eyes that brought us to attention.

And before we could count the days, the apples were ripe and ready. The trees were heavy with the delectable fruit we'd admired and coveted so long and had waited for so patiently.

Now was the time. At last.

Without a word, but with maybe just one little tiny tug by Victorine and there in her hand for all to see was a round, juicy apple.

Instant glee.

And my sisters and our friends, swooshed me up with them, and we attacked the crop with the suddenness of soldiers on a battlefield. The battle cries were squeals of delight. Some of us climbed the tree to better pick the tempting fruit. Such fun it was. Noisy with laughter. Frantic with picking. But so short-lived.

The owner appeared on the double to shoo us away. "Stop, stop. All of you stop picking my apples. At once."

Everyone scattered. Like autumn leaves blown in a gale.

All but me. I was frozen on a lower limb of the apple tree.

The irate fruit owner grabbed my arm. "You've stolen my apples!"

My lips were paralyzed. My voice dead. But I spread my empty hands so he could see they held no forbidden fruit.

"I cannot have you stealing my apples!"

I glanced around for my sisters and friends to come to my rescue. Or at least share the blame and suffer the consequences with me. No one in sight. All had vanished.

Mr. Neighbor looked for them, too. And when they were not to be seen, his face turned red and he held my arm tighter. "I cannot have you stealing my apples," he repeated, his voice still scary. "We're going to the police station. Right now!"

I heard his growl and felt his jerk as he pulled me from my frozen position in the tree and hustled me to the police station a half block away, so a policeman could order me in a stern voice not to steal any apples ever again.

I never did. But I don't know about my sisters and their friends.

I do know now, what I didn't know then, that Mr. Neighbor wished I'd pulled myself free of him and taken off in a frantic dash to join the other thieves, so he wouldn't have to drag me to the police station. He didn't really want to do that to a lone, frightened, pretty, little seven-year-old girl. Especially with the police officers looking askance at him.

But it was very effective.

✳   ✳   ✳   ✳

After several years, I was totally bilingual, which eased the pain of being a misfit in school. But my reading was something else.

A one-eye-at-a-time trick I'd discovered worked fairly well, but reading was still a laborious, blurry process. No way for me to become a happy, well-rounded pupil.

But the true mystery was why I couldn't explain the situation, or even reveal its existence to anyone in authority. Why did I keep my affliction a secret? Why couldn't I tell *Maman?* I wasn't sure.

Perhaps, if Papa were still here—if Papa—I might—well, if he knew about my secret, I might not—I shuddered—I might not be his favorite any more. No. I would always be papa's favorite. Always. Until the end of the world.

Anyway, after Papa died, I couldn't bother *Maman* with my problem. She was too busy with everything. She didn't even have time to cry.

But one day at school a nurse noticed me. She stopped at my desk.

"Why are you squinting, Claire?" she asked, not unkindly.

"I didn't know I was squinting."

"Yes. You were squinting. Come with me. I will examine your eyes."

Her examination was simple enough. She lifted a twenty-five cent coin, told me to close one eye, and asked. "What have I in my hand?"

"A quarter."

"Fine. Now close the other eye."

The same question. And the same answer. "A quarter."

"Excellent. Your vision is good."

The poor nurse didn't know about my one-eye-at-a-time trick. And of course I was unable to tell her. She should have asked me some more questions. She should have had a better examination. She should have known I was unable to speak up. She should have suspected I couldn't reveal a secret without some help. She should have known.

In my innocence, I was bravely optimistic that someone, someday, would understand my eye defect and correct the dilemma. But while still a child, my worse nightmare was that my own children one far distant day could have the same problem and I might not find out soon enough to solve it for them.

So for the time being, in the classroom, I played a special role, a disruptive and compulsive one. I became a clown. Not the way clever Victorine entertained us at home, but with a compulsion to lightness, in a happy-go-lucky, clumsy, stupid, clown way.

I compensated for my slow reading by acting up, disturbing the class, whether I was trying to focus on a book or not. Just any old time. Or every old time. I was the life of the classroom. Always. I was active before class even started. I caused such a commotion Sister sent me to the cloakroom to wait for everyone to be seated before I could join the class.

Many years later, with a lively flock of my own, I remembered all those problems I'd caused my favorite teacher. I wrote her a letter and asked for her forgiveness.

Her answer to me: "Claire, you are the only pupil I remember fondly. You were never mean, only very lively!"

But way back then, I thought if I were not the clown, someone might suspect my despair. Which, of course, I secretly, or subconsciously, certainly desperately, wished someone would hurry up and suspect.

So childhood was not always a blissful state. But that could not change the blissful way I felt about my family. The fault of my personal reading problem certainly could never fall on the shoulders of any member of my beloved family.

But I knew I wasn't exactly like all the other pretty Tétreau sisters who were so perfect and capable and artistic and popular. They could sew and dance and paint beautifully. And read easily with a smooth, articulate delivery. In two languages.

And they could sing in pure, sweet, harmonious voices.

But I sang, too. *Maman*, herself, taught all of us. *Maman* was a wonderful singer. A deep, rich contralto. When we were on our family outings, *Maman* kept us singing, both coming and going. If kids are singing, they aren't squabbling, nor teasing, nor jumping up and down, nor tweaking one another. *Maman* had us singing all the time. I loved to sing. I was good at it. But I was not the best. I was never the very best in anything at our house, except in Papa's eyes. I know he always thought I was the prettiest.

Oh, Papa. But already, his dear face had become difficult for me to remember.

CHAPTER 6

▼

I understood full well my older sisters were teenagers, sophisticates, who knew everything anyone needed to know about the ways of the world, who were adept at all activities necessary for happiness, including—the newest and most exciting—being especially popular with the boys.

I thought all my older sisters were *marveleuse*. My idols.

But how did they feel about the three baby sisters, born after the two boys? Numbers Ten, Eleven and Twelve. Claire, Adrienne and Louise, who did little to lessen the household's monstrous workload. And the ones who had to be constantly watched.

Well, I don't know how the older sisters felt.

I do know everyone adored *Bébé* Louise. Our towhead. A person just couldn't help loving Louise. And at the same time secretly feel sad because Louise never knew our dear papa, hadn't even seen him. Not once. Never sat on his lap while he ate his dinner. I suspect we all wanted to atone for her loss. So Louise was always special.

But how did anyone know what traumas caused other siblings to suffer? In the same way, I think no one in the family had the slightest suspicion I was miserable in school, except when I was singing. Feelings were often secret.

What about Antoinette, our Number One?

Did Antoinette, in the beloved and exalted position of all first borns, suffer continuously, as her special Number One role eroded, one baby at a time? The newest Tétreau baby always became the most beloved. Like clockwork, Antoinette was usurped of her coveted position. Repeatedly. Was that a secret trauma she kept hidden from everyone, possibly herself included?

I don't know. Sometimes she did seem to be in a world of her own.

But she made friends, really good friends, all over. Lots and lots of friends, who meant everything to her. Maybe even more than eleven younger siblings ever could. She constantly wrote letters to those friends. And her pen pals around the world. She bought presents for them. Or fashioned gifts with her own hands. Could eleven little brothers and sisters have been a few too many for Antoinette? Too fast?

I don't know.

I do know her day off from work at the doctors' office was her turn to baby-sit, and sometimes she was a tiny bit scary for the little ones. Partly because she wrote letters all day. If we made any noise or came into the house and disturbed her, she made us kneel down in a corner of the room.

And sometimes, one of us would ask, "Can we get up now, Toni?"

"You asked, so now you will stay longer in the corner," Toni answered, without looking up or stopping her letter-writing. She wasn't mean about it, just strict.

But if we didn't ask, she might forget and leave us there in the corner forever. So we always ended up asking.

One haunting day, Adrienne and I put our dear little Louise inside a large 'traveling trunk' in the back yard. For no real reason. Just for something clever to do. When we decided she'd been in there long enough, neither of us could open the lid.

We tried and tried. Separately and together. No luck. I began to choke from holding my own breath. I felt fear crawling all over me and rubbed my hands together to make it go away. It didn't budge. Finally, desperation set in.

"We'd better get Louise out of there. Right now," Adrienne said.

"I know. I know."

"We'll call Toni to help us," Adrienne said.

"We can't. She'll kill us." I said, quaking.

"We have to."

I knew Adrienne was right.

So we yelled for help and Toni came running and saved *Bébé* Louise.

Adrienne and I ended up in the corner, all right. Louise, too. We were there so long we fell asleep. And Toni finished her letter-writing with no further problems.

But I never really understood why Toni liked to write letters better than she liked watching over the three littlest ones. But the important thing, on her days off, she always did her allotted time with us. Always. She didn't complain. She was always there.

And she did save Louise from suffocating in the trunk.

What about Bertha? What about Laurette? What about Victorine? Well, no one ever had to worry about Victorine.

But did they ever take special walks with *Maman* as I did? And still not be able to ask for help? Like me? Or be able to follow through with decisive action? Or accept responsibility when a situation required it?

For instance. When Dr. Miller, our dentist, told me I had a bad bite that needed to be straightened and he would fix it, I was pleased for his offer, but I couldn't show my pleasure or say anything. I said nothing. Naturally, he concluded I wasn't interested, so the subject was dropped. And the bad bite was never repaired.

So why did I always wait for others to make the decisions and instigate the plans? Simple enough. Because I never had to learn otherwise.

Was I the only one? What about Marguerite? What was in her heart and mind and soul that pulled her from the family into religious seclusion in a strict cloistered convent the second she was old enough? Already, she'd planned her life's direction. Even with a boyfriend patiently waiting the eight years for her to change her mind before her final vows were taken.

Marguerite eventually taught sub-primary and first grade and was a superb teacher. And a dedicated, happy one. But to be cloistered meant after she was eighteen, we rarely saw her.

The first small crack in the family unity.

Think of all the dances and movies and days at the beach she couldn't share with us. To me her leaving the family was a split right down the middle of our private road—through family life—together.

But I learned something later, when that fateful day came: family togetherness was never meant to be forever. The road through family life would get narrower and narrower; the cleft down the middle wider and wider. We'd already lost Papa, hadn't we?

But, how could I dare be sad for myself if to be a cloistered nun was what Marguerite wanted with all her heart? But I didn't look forward to that day when she would finally leave us.

*   *   *   *

Wells Beach was a favorite spot for outings, so when our cousins who owned a lumber company and many trucks volunteered to haul the Tétreau kids and friends and *Maman*, too, for a Sunday at Wells Beach, we didn't waste time getting ready to go.

We grabbed the beach blankets and towels and overflowing picnic baskets and sand buckets and shovels and didn't hide our excitement. We covered the twelve miles quickly and *Maman* had us singing all the way.

Henri jumped down as soon as the truck was parked. *"Venez, Maman. Venez ici. Suivez-moi,"* he said and found a spot to spread a blanket on the hot sand. Here *Maman*, come over here.

Of course, as usual, I didn't think of it at the time, but *Maman* was a heavy woman and she should have had a beach chair. Why were we always so oblivious to her needs? As I look back, I don't think any of us gave *Maman* a thought, unless it concerned our own special desires. Just because she never once thought of her own comfort, or wishes, or necessities, I'm afraid we all were thoughtless, ungrateful children.

Now, these decades later, my remorse catches my breath.

But that particular day at Wells Beach, *Maman* removed her shoes and stockings and asked her sons to hold her hands and with Paul on one side and Henri on the other, she left the blanket and inched her way through the hot sand to the water's edge.

As she soaked her bare feet in the refreshing ocean, she turned to smile at her boys, her *bébés,* first one, then the other, and was caught by the next wave, a rogue, large enough to weaken her balance and topple her over.

"Oh, oh—"

And down she went. The sea water churned and foamed around her.

Paul and Henri struggled to save our mother from the gushing wave and neither released his grip on her hand. Eventually, the current ebbed and *Maman* regained her balance.

"C'était formidable," she laughed.

She relished her unplanned, exhilarating dip in the ocean, and once they knew she was safe, the boys laughed, too.

"That was *marveleuse*," she said, and returned to the blanket to dry, none the worse for the experience, and in truth, quite genuinely pleased with it.

CHAPTER 7

▼

Paul and Henri were lively little boys. I often watched them with their friends as they rolled a tire along the empty street with their 'peggy sticks.' No worry for the boys playing in the road because cars were seldom seen.

And when the boys were tired of their 'peggy sticks,' they chased their many sisters. On the beach or inside the house or anywhere. Everywhere. Our home echoed with their happy thumps and bumps and vibrated with our girlish squeals.

I remember the day Henri chased Adrienne and me with a long stick, much like the pointers Sister used at school. I can still see that long narrow weapon. And being dear, sweet Henri, he held the sharp, pointed end toward himself, so no one would be hurt accidentally.

We laughed and screeched and ran round and round through several rooms. We stopped and started and lunged and side-stepped and swayed. But when Henri cut a corner too closely, and too quickly, the stick hit the door frame and sent the sharp end directly into his stomach.

"Oh, Henri," I moaned. "Henri—"

Bertha took one look and called Dr. Cobb.

Little Louise began to cry.

And while we all wailed and writhed and wrung our hands, Henri casually pulled the stick out of his stomach and said quietly, "I'm all right."

Dr. Cobb came anyway, to be certain all was well.

"No splinters, Dr. Cobb?" Henri joked, as if he hadn't just had a very harrowing few moments.

"No splinters," Dr. Cobb assured, "but you must rest. Hear me, Henri?"

"I hear you."

Henri rested for awhile, but to everyone's relief he was none the worse for the experience.

*   *   *   *

We all saw Dr. Cobb on another summer day. Well, not all of us. But the five youngest. With me were Paul, Henri, Adrienne and Louise. For mass production tonsillectomies.

Paul and Henri were noisy and active and while I waited my turn with Dr. Cobb, I wandered into his library, and admired his many books.

I found Mark Twain's *The Prince and the Pauper* with large, easy-to-see print and sank into a nearby chair and began to read. I found the reading surprisingly easy and Mark Twain's story captivating. The experiences of the elegant prince and the ragged pauper stirred my heart. I hadn't realized a book could be so mesmerizing. The feelings stayed with me.

When I saw the movie years later, with Errol Flynn and Billy and Bobby Mauch, I was enchanted all over again.

And fifty years after that, I discovered an original copy of the book in an antique store. My surprise and delight were obvious to the store owner. She was so moved when she saw the expression on my face as I told her my childhood experience of reading the story in the doctor's office, she handed me the precious book and wouldn't even let me pay for it.

*   *   *   *

In time, Sister gave me another eye test. We were both pleased and relieved about my comprehension, which was well beyond the hoped-for level.

"But Claire, your reading is still too slow," she said. "I want you to take a special course in Speed-Reading."

"All right, I said," deeply grateful for the long-awaited recognition. "All right," I repeated, a bit louder, with a wide smile, thrilled my problem could be corrected.

I took the Speed-Reading course. No luck. I took it a second time. No luck. So, well, what a quandary.

At least I wasn't the clumsy idiot I thought might be the truth about me. That was some consolation.

But not nearly enough.

So I've been forever grateful to *The Prince and the Pauper,* which did more for my reading than twice with the Sister's Speed-Reading course.

*   *   *   *

That year, Christmas was still the same warmly fulfilling holiday it had always been before Papa died.

And the same concerned neighborhood grocer, Mr. Guillemette, secretly filled *Maman's* shopping bag with nuts and large oranges to be stuffed in the stockings of the Tétreau children on Christmas morning.

The family custom was to trim the tree after the little ones were asleep. *Maman* and the older girls completed that activity in a hurry. And on Christmas morning, I was sure, and Adrienne and Louise were also sure, little Jesus Himself had come to our home, put up the tree and decorated it for us.

*   *   *   *

Everyone helped in the Tétreau household. But a long time ago, Papa had negotiated a note, using our home on State Street as collateral. A few years after Papa died, that note came due, and as diligently as *Maman* tried, as conscientious as Rose and Delia were, they could not raise enough to pay off the note.

Just not enough. The task was unconquerable.

Poor *Maman*. She'd been so brave. She'd tried so hard.

The note bearer took over the house.

Our home on State Street was gone.

*   *   *   *

So maybe the house was gone. But no matter. Life kept right on a forward course. *Maman* saw to that.

So, on a pleasant sunny afternoon in May, with a delicate breeze rustling through the elm trees, the Tétreau family moved to a rental triplex not too far away, on Jackson Street. Two large apartments with four bedrooms, one bath and an attic. And under our flat, a small empty bachelor apartment.

While *Maman* and the others checked out the bedrooms upstairs, Adrienne pulled me with her to the bachelor apartment below.

"It isn't locked," she said with a touch of mystery in her words. "It's open," she added and shoved the door wide.

For a second we were speechless. Then Adrienne found her voice. Softly, in a whisper. "Oh, Claire, our new playroom."

I just stared. I thought of Papa's shiny, black, vintage, horse-drawn carriage which had been our special place for such a long time, now left behind in our backyard on State Street.

Adrienne clapped her hands and marched about the empty room, her big eyes bright and her smile broad.

One thing: the room was empty. No furniture. We couldn't do much damage.

And after our ecstatic discovery we joined *Maman* and the others.

The girls would have to share the bedrooms, but we were accustomed to it. We younger ones were all so small we never considered sharing a hardship.

The afternoon we arrived, an amazing white Alaskan husky appeared unannounced from nowhere and decided this place was his home, too. We called him Jocko. And he clearly intended to stay. Our instant watchdog.

That first night in our new home, Rose and Delia couldn't even approach the house because of Jocko, the new guard dog. And no sneaking around him, either. His bark was loud and deep, most convincing. He alerted everyone in the entire neighborhood in his zeal to protect his house.

Adrienne and I loved Jocko. We held him close so our big sisters could enter their new home.

Many times, Adrienne said, "Come on, Claire, let's go for a ride."

And we tied Jocko to our wagon and he dragged us up and down and all around the block. Around and around. And we knew Jocko had just as much fun as we did. And a bit of exercise, too.

Jocko wasn't always beloved. One bitter, blustery winter day, our errant hero kindled a fury no one realized lay dormant in our dear Bertha. She had washed and hung the sheets and family clothes on the lines. A truly significant chore.

And when no one was looking, Jocko tugged and jerked on the frigid sheets until he had pulled the poles down, and the ice-heavy clothes, frozen solid, fell stiffly on the cold, wet, muddy ground.

"Jocko, *tu es méchant*," Bertha yelled. In French because Jocko didn't understand English. *"Méchant, méchant chien."* Bad, bad dog. And her anger was so rare even Jocko got the message.

I particularly remember that clothesline. In the wintertime, when the clothes were finally dry enough, and stiff as steel, we brought them inside and stood them in the kitchen corner to thaw out just exactly enough for perfect ironing.

But our new kitchen no longer had our wonderful black cast iron relic we ran to every morning in the old house to warm our feet. No. We had advanced to a shiny, new, white electric stove, which made the kitchen much larger, but not necessarily a friendly place.

I'd never thought about *Maman* rising in the early hours on State Street to start a fire in that old stove and to feed wood and paper into it, so the flames wouldn't die before all the children had a chance to warm their feet.

Now I think *Maman* must have savored those early mornings in the quiet solitude of that aged kitchen, tending the fire, while twelve children were silent and immobile in the tenderness and bliss of sleep.

But we all loved that ancient stove. Except maybe on that one memorable day we saw a blob of what looked like silver on it. An unknown someone had carelessly put *Maman's* best old wedding present on that hot stove, only to discover later the precious gift, a silver sugar bowl, had been reduced to a silver puddle on the stove.

But who could forget the clean smell of a scrubbed bare wood kitchen floor, and the Saturday evening dinner delight of beans baking in the huge pot. Not me. Not any of us.

I wondered if *Maman* had remembered to bring the potatoes and carrots from the old house. She kept them fresh and cool in a raised foundation of earth down by the cellar stairs. Sometimes vegetables in that cold storage even sprouted there in the dirt. Well, no matter. We always managed to eat well, wherever we lived. Now I wonder how *Maman* did it.

Anyway, she did.

So our new house was different. But our school was the same. Sanford had only one Catholic Parish at that time, St. Ignatius. Just a different route to get there. Not much farther away than our old place.

CHAPTER 8

▼

The spring morning was fresh and invigorating, with a hint of approaching summer on the warm breeze.

While exploring a different neighborhood on Church Street that day, Rose and Victorine passed by a large three story house, a big old white elephant with an encircling screen porch.

The girls stopped short simultaneously and turned back for a double-take of the old house they'd never seen before. The sight electrified them.

"Vickie, 'gard, 'gard. Regard ons la maison pour nous." Look. Look. The house for us.

"I see it. I see it." Vickie's voice was shrill with excitement.

"Did you notice the For Sale sign? Vickie, I absolutely know you're thinking what I'm thinking."

Vickie's head bobbed up and down and the sisters stared at each other and both felt another jab of excitement as their thoughts coincided. There, standing before them, was a mansion of three stories, a big enough white elephant to house the entire Tétreau family. In comfort. And in elegance.

They both inhaled slowly again with the enormity of their thoughts and stopped under one of the graceful shade trees to compose their rapture.

They were quiet, as their decision took hold and wound its way through their minds and hearts. And while they waited for the assimilation, they glanced around the coveted property.

"Look at the massive barn back there." Rose pointed.

"I see it."

"The house on Jackson Street isn't right for us," Rose continued and glanced at Vickie again. They both smiled in secret conspiracy.

Then Rose aimed right at the soul of the matter. "How do you think we should go about buying this beautiful place?"

Vickie was quiet a moment. And stared at her sister again. "Well, we could ask Toni to talk to the doctors. Maybe they could give us some advice. She could tell them we'd like to own this big old white elephant some day and could they help us find out how to go about it."

And that's exactly what happened. Rose spoke to Antoinette. And Antoinette approached the doctors for advice. They learned the selling price was $4,500. Not a bad figure for a three-story mansion. The entire country wallowed in financial disaster since the New York Stock Market crashed last year, so maybe one way or another, something could be worked out.

And something did work out.

Dr. Cobb went to the bank and instructed the loan officer to give Mrs. Tétreau any amount she might need and he would vouch for it, no questions asked.

The answer to everyone's prayers.

Because Rose was right. No one in the Tétreau family really liked the place on Jackson Street. A year and a half was long enough to stay there.

So we moved again.

To our beautiful mansion on Church Street.

*   *   *   *

Moving day was exquisite, with a sky of fleecy clouds. Winds whispered through the pines and stirred their delicate perfume.

Our new home was spacious: six bedrooms, two formal parlors, a formal dining room with a built in buffet, a table that would seat twelve comfortably, a Tiffany chandelier above.

Also, an enormous kitchen with an oak table large enough for all of us, a huge pantry, a laundry room with a doorway to the backyard garage and barn and a stairway to the hay loft. And from there, a door to the upstairs bedrooms.

Adrienne and I were ecstatic. We ran up and down and all around. We found four ways to get to the upper floors: one staircase had an ornate balustrade going to the front bedrooms. A second stairway led to what turned out to be our third floor bedroom. Another was between the kitchen and an extra room—an office or den. Then stairs in the barn led to the back bedrooms and the loft.

This lovely home was just the right size for our large, active family. It had belonged to a doctor, and the next door neighbor was understandably upset that twelve children so close might invade her space.

"This used to be an elite area, and now all those children—" she seemed to be crying out. But she was too polite to actually say the words.

Jocko didn't come with us. He stayed with his house. I guess that place on Jackson Street truly was his.

But *Maman* had a cat, Tallulah, which that elite neighbor tried to win over with special catnip. But Tallulah remained forever faithful to her dear Aurelie.

We had many pleasant neighbors on Church Street.

Mrs. Bessie Yarlick lived in a yellow house at the end of our block and stopped me once to say, "Claire, please tell your mother that my invalid husband sits all day at the window and has much pleasure watching the swarm of children go in and out and around your home."

"All right, Mrs. Yarlick, I'll tell her that."

"Mr. Yarlick and I are both so grateful to all of you. There is never a dull moment."

Mrs. Yarlick was certainly correct about that.

Maman spoke only French and Mrs. Yarlick often said to her own children, "Go play with the Tétreau kids and learn to speak French. You'll be glad of it someday."

Mrs. Yarlick also had an English bulldog named Duke that liked the hubbub and excitement of our home, and she said, "I don't mind if Duke eats your hash instead of the steak I have for him, but please don't speak French to him because now he doesn't understand me any more."

We discovered the little neighbor lady directly across the street was petrified of our Maine thunder storms. Whenever she heard one coming she hid in a closet, afraid to emerge until after an hour or so of quiet.

So I said to her, "Why don't you come over to our house the next time a storm hits and you can talk to *Maman* and ignore the thunder and lightning. After all, *Maman* gave birth to me in a blizzard, you know." Once I learned that fact myself, I reminded people whenever possible.

When the very next storm struck, our neighbor ran across the street to sit with *Maman* in the soft chairs in one of our parlors. Within ten minutes poor overworked *Maman* was fast asleep. The little neighbor lady just sat there and marveled, as the storm blustered.

But I know for a fact she never cowered in her closet during a Maine storm again.

At the same time our family moved to the mansion, and after everyone's urging, *Maman* finally gave up Papa's Tailor Shop. Sad in a way, but best for everyone, especially Rose and Delia who were happy to quit the cleaning and pressing and go to work with Laurette in the mills.

When the burden of keeping Papa's shop open was removed and we settled in our new home on Church Street, an unexpected aura of relief sifted through the house, a peace, as though we had at last found our proper place.

*   *   *   *

Every morning as usual we went to early Mass before school. If we ran the noisy short cut through the alley between the Fire Station and a large warehouse, the church and school were only three blocks from our new home. We had to time our run through the alley carefully so we were not blown away when the seven o'clock whistle indicated all was well. That happened once. And once was enough. So we timed our departure carefully. And ran as fast as we could.

I guess I was what could be called a reluctant pupil. Going to school was what I had to do, not what I ever really wanted to do.

But at age four, our dear little *Bébé* Louise was ready and anxious for school.

"Where do you think you're going, Louise?" Vickie asked one morning, as the Tétreau group was out the door and on the way to school.

"Je vais à l'école avec vous," Louise answered. I'm going to school with you.

"Does Bertha know?" asked Vickie.

"She's very busy right now. So I'm going to school with you."

"You are not."

"I already know my numbers. And some of my letters."

By that time, we were half way down the block. Bertha had watched from the doorway and knew what Louise had in mind.

"Well, okay," Adrienne said, "but hurry. We're almost late."

I wondered who would walk home with Louise when Sister discovered the new four-year-old pupil in the class.

Sister didn't waste any time.

"Just who are you?" she asked at once.

"I'm Louise Tétreau," our baby sister said, in clear, positive tones, and smiled and bobbed her blonde head.

I could almost hear the Sister sigh. Another Tétreau starting shool. Well, nothing unusual about that.

"All right, come along," Sister said. "You stay until noon. Then you go home. And remain there."

We always went home for lunch, anyway, so what was the difference?

Sister gave Louise a seat, a pencil and a piece of paper.

But after lunch, four-year-old determined Louise followed us back to school.

Sister said. "Well, if Louise wants to attend school that much, we'll let her stay."

And Louise stayed.

And her school work was always brilliant.

Louise eventually became an artist, especially excelled in painting seascapes, and through the years won many prizes in that category. She became well known as The Seagull Lady, which title always made me smile, because I knew it was meant to be complimentary.

Louise had no formal training in either art or music, and as well as being The Seagull Lady, she had the voice of an opera diva. *Maman* had a singing teacher for Louise, but would not allow her youngest *bébé* to leave home to discover and train her wonderful potential. Never.

Maman was a very humble person, who had the deepest respect of the community, even in the neighboring towns, but she made all the decisions, ruled and protected her girls with a steel arm and kept her *bébés* forever safe at home.

When the time was right, she planned each daughter would find a nice French Catholic boy to marry and settle down. Except Marguerite, of course, who would become an Ursaline Nun.

Sometimes I wondered what *Maman* would have done, if she'd had ten boys and two girls, instead of the vice versa.

CHAPTER 9

▼

Maman loved to walk, to visit friends and relatives, especially our *Tante Agathe et Oncle Albert* who lived with their children about a mile from our home.

"*Maman*, can Adrienne and I go with you?" I asked each time. And *Maman* always smiled and reached out her hands to us. And off we went together.

Adrienne and I enjoyed playing with the cousins while Maman visited with our aunt and uncle. I especially loved their backyard. The hillside seemed to go down forever into a thick forest of lush pine trees. The wind whistled softly through them and I usually slipped away from Adrienne and the cousins after awhile to sit on the porch swing and listen. And daydream. Such peace. I hated to leave.

*   *   *   *

Time high-stepped right along, but the economy of the 1930's had not improved. The Tétreau family continued to stick it out together, with the help of the Goodall Mills and the sisters who were weavers there, plus Antoinette who continued to work for the good doctors.

But no one really suspected, as we probably should have, that Victorine would be the one to designate the path most of the family would eventually travel, even though *Maman* was forever the final decision maker. Maybe we weren't surprised Vickie was the instigator, but no one in the beginning, not even *Maman*, could have guessed the actual course she created.

The direction began innocently enough, when Vickie was no older than thirteen or fourteen. Such a creative little girl she was. Such an undeniable talent she possessed. Her passion for it consumed her: the desire to clip, shape, wave, to coif hair. Anyone's hair. Everyone's hair.

She began on her own and advanced to her friends and the willing members of the family, and eventually to Cousin Albert, and by word of mouth, throughout the neighborhood.

Vickie walked to her various appointments until one day *Maman* thought that wasn't safe and right then and there made the decision to redesign our office-den into a beauty parlor for Vickie.

"Alors, la clientèle de Vickie *peut venir ici,"* Maman said. Then clients can come here.

"Yes!" Vickie agreed. "Where my equipment and supplies are. I won't have to carry everything all over town. Yes, let my customers come here."

Voilà. Vickie's beauty salon.

The shine in Vickie's eyes was bright.

And later when her business prospered, Maman decided the large front parlor would make a better, bigger salon.

As always, in every situation, no matter what, *Maman* had the final word. And in time, because she so deemed, the large front parlor became the new salon.

*   *   *   *

Young Cousin Albert was Vickie's favorite model. Whenever he visited, she persuaded him to cooperate, so she could practice her finger waves and any new techniques that inspired her, on his thick mop of black hair.

"Oh, Albert, how great to see you," she always cooed. "Come into the salon." Come into my parlor, my den, my web. "I want to show you—I need to practice—"

"Vickie, do I always have to?"

"Yes. We'll give you lunch."

"Will lunch be something delicious *Tante* Aurelie has made today?"

"*Mais oui. Certainment.* Yes, it is. It's a surprise. But only if you let me work on your hair."

"Well, if you promise to wash it all out."

"Of course, I will," Vickie said. "Don't I always?"

Albert nodded and flopped in a chair in our new beauty salon, no longer our front parlor.

And hours later, when Vickie finished, she washed Albert's hair and returned it to its original style.

However, one fateful day, Albert was not so lucky. He sat through a brand new procedure with a special contraption standing innocently beside him.

"What is that?" he pointed and asked with a quiver in his voice and his eyes wide. "It looks like a milking machine."

"Well, it isn't a milking machine. It's a wave-making machine. I simply roll up your hair, your perfect hair, in these little rollers, with a special solution which you'll be able to smell—not a bad scent at all—and turn on the heat and *voilà*—curls."

Albert blinked a few times in astonishment. "You'll wash the curls out afterwards? After you practice? Like you always do?"

"Of course. Like I always do."

So Albert sat through hours of agony as Vickie practiced with the new wave machine.

When the operation was finally completed, Albert's hair was indeed curly. Very curly. Extraordinarily curly.

He took one look in the mirror and began to yell.

"Wash it out! Wash it out! Hurry, Vickie. *Vite. Vite.* Fast."

Everyone in the house raced to the home salon to see what caused the commotion.

Oh, Cousin Albert had curly hair, all right.

We were shocked and amused at the sight of him, but retained our serious expressions as much as we could—which wasn't really very much. We didn't laugh outright, but our faces burst with smiles and our eyes danced with hilarity.

Albert was a sight.

We backed away with our laughter barely muffled to leave Vickie alone with her problem.

She scrubbed Albert's hair and scalp at least three times, maybe four. Vigorously. But the new process was for permanent waves. So, of course, the curls wouldn't go away.

"This machine really works," Vickie said pleasantly to the screeching Albert. "I think the waves truly are permanent. Don't you? Until your hair grows out, that is."

"Vickie!" Albert wailed again. "You didn't say they were going to be permanent! You said you were just practicing."

"Yes, Albert, I was testing the machine. And it works just fine. So stop hollering or the neighbors will be over here to see what's going on."

"Then chop off my hair! Just get your scissors out and cut my hair! All of it. Right now."

So Vickie cut Albert's hair. Almost all of it.

The family laughed, secretly and discreetly, because Albert looked like a porcupine peeping out from under the cap he insisted on wearing. He wore that cap every day, indoors and out, until his hair grew and could be trimmed again to his satisfaction.

We thought of him as Albert The Porcupine for a long time. And a bit of laughter always spilled over with the thought.

Vickie's business continued to flourish with the permanent wave machine added. Rose and Laurette were intrigued enough with the details to leave their jobs at the mills to join Vickie in her home salon. Very quickly, Rose became an exceptionally artistic *coiffeuse*, herself.

More and more customers arrived and to handle the thriving business, the other Tétreau sisters, one by one, left the mills to follow in Vickie's footsteps.

Not Antoinette, of course. She stayed with Dr. Cobb and Dr. Ross.

Not Marguerite.

But even our he-man brother, Paul, became a hair stylist.

I think everyone was surprised at the direction Vickie chose for us and the ease with which we all joined together.

And when I reached the age of twelve, I sterilized combs and swept the floor after school. When Adrienne and Louise were older, they did the menial work, too.

So with *Maman's* help, Vickie was the one who led us all down her chosen path. We became a family of hairdressers. Eight of us, eventually. Including me.

I always hated it.

My dream was to become an airline stewardess.

CHAPTER 10

▼

We were at last content in our new home on Church Street. Adrienne and I were pleased with our third story bedroom. Just the two of us. We both preferred good, fresh air and our windows were seldom closed at night.

In winter, however, we had to shut the heater vents in our room to keep the heat downstairs.

Maman made us long-sleeved flannel nightgowns with caps to match. And we had plenty of blankets. So we were never cold.

But the first thing each morning, I said, "Adrienne, get up, get up. Close the windows. And don't forget to shut the stairway door."

And one of us always jumped out of bed, closed the windows and ran to shut the stairway door.

And when we were dressed, we raced downstairs to a kitchen warm from the coal-burning furnace.

In late spring, everyone helped to remove the storm windows, all carefully marked so they would be ready to install in the proper places in November before the winter storms began again. The storm windows were a great help to the furnace which had a large house to heat.

But I liked the cold winters. Probably because I was born, on that memorable birth-date blizzard, with a built-in affinity for winter weather.

So when that first hot, sticky, humid summer stifled Adrienne and me in our third floor bedroom, we were desperate.

"Let's throw our mattress out the window and sleep outside," Adrienne suggested, always ready with a plan.

"Let's," I agreed, always willing to follow the leader, whoever it might be, whatever the plot.

So Adrienne and I heaved our mattress out the third story window. Not exactly an easy task, but together we managed.

"Nothing can be worse than this awful, stuffy heat," Adrienne wailed; however, we discovered fighting the mosquitoes outside and lugging our mattress back up two flights of stairs—after the mosquitoes won the battle—were in fact, worse than the humid heat.

We should have known.

∗   ∗   ∗   ∗

Our new yard had a mature McIntosh apple tree that produced a bumper crop every other year. For whatever reason, the year following the huge harvest, was always a lean one.

We loved those apples. Apple pie. Applesauce. Apple cider. Apple butter. Apple everything. *Maman's* magic with those apples was endless.

And always hovering in the back of my mind was my forced march to the police station that time past when we lived on

State Street and apples were stolen mysteriously from our neighbor's tree and I turned out to be the only thief.

Our Bartlett pear tree produced so much fruit the laden branches almost touched the ground. With every Tétreau picking at will, I believe not even one pear was ever left long enough on the tree to fully ripen. And all these years later, I still like my pears a bit on the green side.

Many times I climbed that pear tree, perched myself on a branch, ate green pears and read my books for hours. Yes, after 'The Prince and the Pauper', I discovered I liked to read.

I was often accused of hiding in the branches of that pear tree to escape washing the dishes, but someone always called me in.

"Claire, *nous te voyons dans l'arbre. C'est à toi de laver la vaisselle. Il faut te dépecher et entrer à la maison.*" We see you in that tree. It's your turn to wash the dishes. You'd better hurry up and get in here.

So, if I truly ever had a plan to avoid doing the dishes, it never worked.

And I can still visualize our five gallon milk can on the back steps with the frozen cream pushed a foot above the top of the can.

On Church Street, our milkman delivered milk every other day. Each time he removed the empty five gallon can and replaced it with a fresh, full one.

I don't remember where we kept the milk in summer, but five gallons didn't last long anyway, so I'm sure it rarely had time to sour out there on the back porch.

*   *   *   *

After six years, *Maman* and I returned to the old family grocery store when we lived on State Street, to finally pay Mr. Guillemette for the charges *Maman* made for groceries after Papa died.

A few days later, for *Maman's* honesty and integrity, she received a gracious note from Mr. Guillemette: "Thank you to our dear friend. It was our pleasure, Mrs. Tétreau."

Everyone who knew *Maman* was impressed. She was a determined, young, single parent, both creative and enterprising and certainly devoted and hard-working.

She understandably ruled our lives with a strong will. But at the same time she attempted always to make life easier for her children. With ten girls, I'm sure she was wise to hold tight reins.

Even so, sometimes I believe—I'm afraid a few of us were left with—well, at least I think I was left with—very little will of my own.

*   *   *   *

One autumn day, after a devastating summer forest fire, six of us piled in the truck and were off to pick wild blueberries in those same charred woods.

The blueberries seemed to have thrived after the disastrous fire and the lush patch overflowed with berries the size of cherries.

We filled our baskets and pails and stuffed our mouths at the same time.

"Your lips are blue," Henri said to me.

"So are yours." I laughed and knew my tongue, my fingers and hands were also stained.

Oh, we all had such a great time, picking and eating those blueberries.

And when the many containers were full, Maman beamed, I suppose already with thoughts about blueberry muffins and blueberry *crêpes* and blueberry—lots of things.

"Eh bien, alors, est vous prês de retourner à la maison?" Well then, is everybody ready to go home?

We nodded and headed for the truck with our overflowing baskets and pails, when a car pulled up beside us and stopped. Two men, serious and stern, stepped out and approached slowly.

We watched them. And waited.

"We're sorry you did all this work for nothing," one of the men said. "We're here to tell you—because of that big forest fire we had last summer—the berries are now contaminated. You must leave them here. Don't dare eat them."

I was stunned and crestfallen to hear the report. It sounded very official to me. Fortunately, *Maman* and my brothers knew the ways of poachers.

"Is that so?" Paul said and sauntered over to one of the baskets still on the ground, grabbed a handful of blueberries and popped them all in his mouth. He chomped down on them and the juice overflowed from his big mouthful and slowly slipped down his chin.

The two men realized they were not talking to innocents and slowly backed away, slid into their car and drove off fast. Empty-handed.

For a few seconds, I wondered if Paul would drop dead from contaminated blueberries—and the rest of us, one by one, after him. But when I realized those dishonest men simply wanted to steal our berries, all I said was, "Paul, your chin is blue."

And everyone laughed.

We sang all the way home.

CHAPTER 11

▼

One summer, Vickie, in her early teens, attended a hair-style convention in Boston. While there, she visited Filene's Department Store to ask for a job as hairdresser.

Absolutely not, was the positive answer. I suppose because Vickie was too young and therefore inexperienced.

"Well, may I use one of your booths? Just work on my own?"

She was granted her request and her hair-styling was so outstanding one of their regular customers asked to have her next hair appointment with 'the new girl.'

So Vickie was hired after all, and Filene's displayed a large sign VICKIE FROM MAINE in bold letters to advertise the arrival of their clever, new stylist.

But after two weeks, our little hairdresser announced she was leaving.

"I'm sorry. I have to go home now. I'm only in Boston for a vacation."

Yes. Time to go home to Sanford. Where her heart really was. Where her own clients lived.

I don't know how Filene's Department Store reacted to Vickie's abrupt departure, but I suspect the large sign, VICKIE FROM MAINE, was eliminated as quickly as possible.

Our Vickie was a very colorful individual.

One morning a stranger came into our salon in Sanford and claimed she'd heard Vickie was the best stylist in town.

"I want my hair colored and styled," she said to Vickie. "Something new and different. Something dashing and eye-catching. Something that will make my husband's eyes sparkle."

"All right," Vickie said with a smile, "that's exactly what we will do, something new and different and dashing and eye-catching. Something that will make your husband's eyes sparkle."

And without a second lost, Vickie got busy.

When the customer was out of the dryer, ready for the comb-out, Vickie said, "I believe we have something unusual here—something very colorful. I think you'll love your—" Vickie smiled innocently, "—your bright red hair."

"Bright red? Oh, no, you didn't. Not bright red," the woman gasped.

"*Voilà*, there you are."

The woman glanced in the mirror just as her husband entered the salon to fetch her, and they both saw the vision in the mirror at the same time.

The husband's eyes did sparkle. In pleasure and surprise. And the wife was silenced at once by his obvious admiration.

After that, she returned every month for her make-over.

In six months, she handed Vickie a key. "I cannot drive from Washington every month, so I have a Beauty Salon all ready for you in D.C."

Vickie's eyes widened, but she said nothing, and the lady continued. I guarantee the wives of government men will be your clients."

"But—"

"Here is the key."

By then, Vickie had gathered her wits. "Thank you so much, but I really don't want to leave Maine and my family."

And that was the end of it.

At the age of seventeen, Vickie entered a cut-and-style competition. "I call my style 'The Pinwheel,' she told the family.

Her 'Pinwheel' was examined with great interest by all the judges, but she didn't win. So imagine our reaction when the next issue of 'Hairdresser Magazine' featured Vickie's pinwheel as the newest style—only secretly stolen by another hairdresser.

Also imagine our reaction the following year when Vickie—just eighteen—won the International Grand Prize for hair-cutting and style at the National Hair Convention in New York City.

The entire Tétreau family was proud of Vickie, but secretly I was relieved I was not expected to enter any of the competitions Vickie thrived on. Because I could never be as capable as my sisters, I even dreaded the competition that existed among members of our family.

I suppose, being one of the three little ones, I shouldn't have compared my incapability to the many accomplishments of my seven older sisters. I don't really know. But my heart simply wasn't in it.

And as long as I was never going to be an airline stewardess, I thought I should have gone to work in the mills.

＊   ＊   ＊   ＊

Our mother was proud of her large family, her bevy of ten comely girls and two handsome sons.

When she decided the time was right for a family portrait, I was twelve.

"We're all going to have our pictures taken," she announced at dinner one night. "We already have an appointment with the Olan Mills Studio. So get yourselves ready for Saturday morning."

The news was exciting and we spent the next few days worrying about what to wear and waiting our turn for Vickie or Rose to set our hair fashionably.

For the main family portrait, Paul and Henri both wore a suit and tie and sat in the front row, one at each end with *Maman* in the center with the two little ones, Adrienne and Louise, on either side of her. Lined up in the second row, were the remaining sisters, standing in a slight profile—the only time I was grouped with the big girls.

Every hair was carefully coiffed. Every dress was perfect. Every face wore a smile. The faint pastel, fake backdrop of an ancient Italian—or maybe Greek—portico and other foreign-type edifices, added to the grandeur.

We posed for hours. Individually and as a family. Finally, everything was complete. We thanked the photographer and went home.

I still have the wonderful photograph of us all together, and remember the many years the individual photos graced the walls of our Church Street mansion.

But a second chapter emerged years later. The place was Biddeford, Maine. Time for another portrait. At least Louise and I thought so.

"An Olan Mills Studio is here in Biddeford," Louise said. "Why don't you and I go there for an up-dated portrait?"

"Just the two of us?"

"Why not?"

Well, exactly. Why not?

I always liked those old photographs and little Louise was only six years old when they were taken. A new one was due.

So we made an appointment and dolled ourselves up to go.

And then came the shock.

I was at my most gracious and said pleasantly to the photographer, "We visited your studio in Sanford a number of years ago, only then it was our entire family."

"Oh, yes, I remember the family," he said. His voice was curt and a bit of anger drifted through to us.

"Oh?"

"I was so furious with all of you that day."

"What do you mean?" I was truly stunned by his confession and attitude.

He was undaunted. "Well, here came these well-groomed, beautiful young ladies. Your coiffures, to be expected, were all perfect in the short style of the time. Not a hair misplaced, even on the little girls." He paused, but neither Louise nor I could speak, and he went right on.

"And not one of you selfish girls," he continued, "had bothered to prepare your mother's hair."

Silence.

Louise and I were not ready for the tirade we heard, and the photographer hadn't finished.

"So you don't even remember. Well, I chided you at the time, to repair the *faux pas*."

At that moment, I began to recall that Vickie had moved quickly and easily fixed *Maman's* naturally curly hair.

But the photographer intended to review the incident in its entirety.

"I was not about to snap a single picture until your mother's hair was as perfect as all the rest of you."

I glanced at Louise and inwardly moaned. A house full of hairdressers and not one soul, not even one, thought of *Maman* that day.

And after the photographer brought the episode back to life again, it rumbled around in my heart, even though I was not old enough or skilled enough in hairdressing, at the time, to take the blame. And certainly Louise, who was only six, should not feel ashamed.

Still, I will never again forget our unforgivable behavior that left such an imprint on this man, this photographer, that he recognized us, only two of us, instantly, and recalled so vividly. And was still angry about it.

I wondered why children could be so thoughtless. And then I remembered—because they were children.

CHAPTER 12

▼

The nineteen-thirties, heavy and dreary in financial depression, with no television, no computers, no cell phones to help pass the time of day, were vitalized by the Golden Age of Hollywood movies, the glamorous stars, the handsome leading men, the cheap tickets, (but no pop corn).

Great epics, like *Gone With The Wind*; comedies like *It Happened One Night*, with Clark Gable and Claudette Colbert; musicals with Fred Astaire and Ginger Rogers; the singing of Nelson Eddy and Jeannette MacDonald. We always sang right along with Nelson and Jeannette.

And the darling of everyone, curly-haired child movie star, Shirley Temple, beloved around the world.

And in 1934, before the days of in vitro techniques which made multiple births no longer rare—the Dionne quintuplets were born in Canada.

"Five of them!" Adrienne said, excited. "All girls."

"But there are ten Tétreau girls," I said.

"Oh, Claire, we're all different ages."

I shrugged. Oh, well. I, too, thought along with the rest of the world—the Dionne quintuplets were all cute babies and did much to lift the depressed mode of the day.

And the most interesting part to us, much later, in 1957, when the Dionne quintuplets were twenty-three years old, one of *Maman's* many Langlois relatives in Canada, Philippe Langlois, married Cecile Dionne, one of those famous quintuplets.

I thought that bit of news was exciting, even though we really never knew most of *Maman's* Langlois relatives in Canada.

* * * *

A song came out in 1937 about ten pretty girls in a village school, five were blondes, four brunettes and one was a saucy little red head. The boy in the song loved them all. They grew up, the boy left school and at twenty-one, he married the girl whose hair was red—

Oh, there were ten pretty girls, the chorus echoed again and again. Ten Pretty Girls.

I personally thought for sure this song was written especially for us.

But, of course I was wrong again.

* * * *

In summer, our Sunday turkey dinners were very special. The dining room table was carefully set and the overhead brightly-colored Tiffany chandelier added to the happy atmosphere.

Paul and Henri killed the big turkey. *Maman* singed the feathers over a fire—a dangerous chore. Then, with berry clips, the big girls removed the pinfeathers. When all was ready for the oven, *Maman* poured a bottle of homemade beer over the bird in the roaster, which later made the gravy scrumptious.

Warm bread with such a delicious aroma, came straight from the oven, and four-layer strawberry shortcake from *Maman's* favorite recipe was dessert.

How we loved those turkey dinners. I will always remember the camaraderie we shared on those Sunday afternoons.

I think now, if only, for just a moment, we could all return to childhood on one of those Sundays. With the turkey dinner in the dining room.

If only.

But the way of the world is never backward. Never at a standstill. Always forward. Forever. At its own pace. In its own direction.

Still—

*   *   *   *

"Beach day! Beach day!" Henri called through the house one glorious summer day, and everyone whooped and hollered and scurried to get ready. As we always did on beach day.

Well, not everyone. Just those who were not otherwise occupied with work at the mills or with the doctors or with Vickie and her salon.

So we crowded in the family Oldsmobile with our beach towels and blankets, clam-digging equipment, and were singing by the time we were half-way down the block. And *Maman* was quick to tell us what great singers we were.

I knew we headed for Wells Beach because of the clam-digging shovels, the buckets and pots for the clams in the car. And as we approached we heard the roar of the surf and the smell of the salty air and nearby clam flats. Nothing was ever more exciting.

We parked and scrambled out of the Olds and together searched the crowded sands for a good place for our blankets.

"Over here," Paul called.

And we hurried to his chosen place. Paul always found us a perfect spot on the warm sand.

When all was secure, everyone headed for the surf with our cot-sized mattress covers. If we wet the covers and ran very fast down the beach, they filled with air.

"Tie a knot! Quick!" Paul said and *voilà,* a flotation large enough for two or more.

We surfed for hours. And it was more exciting than if we had owned regular surf boards. Anyway, I thought so. Adrienne and I rode tandem and couldn't get enough of it. Sublime. Heaven.

And later, at low tide, *Maman,* the boys and the three of us younger ones ambled to the clam flats on the bayside to gather clams for two delicious meals: New England clam chowder and huge individual servings of steamed clams.

With so many of us, it didn't take long to find the air holes in the mud. And Paul, with a clam hoe, dug up the tasty little gems.

When the large porcelain pots were full, Paul and Henri carried them to the car. The route was not easy on bare feet because of the blistering sand and the hot pebbles on the parking lot. So once the clams were stashed in the Olds, the boys made a quick dash to the ocean to cool and wash their muddied feet. Then back to the blankets, rumpled and sandy, and the surf again.

What bliss.

All this time, the older Tétreau girls strolled the beach.

When Laurette saw a handsome young man with a bleeding gash on his head, she grabbed his hand and ran with him straight to *Maman*.

"*Maman, Maman,* he's hurt," Laurette called as they approached, "we have to help him."

Maman took over. As Laurette knew she would.

"Get some fresh water to wash the wound and some kidney beans," *Maman* said to Paul. Then she turned to the wounded young man.

"*Comment vous appellez vous?*"

"My name is Armand."

"*Comment avez-vous fait mal à la tête?*" So how did you hurt your head?

Armand closed his eyes for a moment and took a deep breath. "Well, I guess I was showing off for the girls," He said and glanced sheepishly at Laurette. "And I hit my head on a piece of driftwood."

At that moment, Paul returned with the fresh water and beans—where he could have found beans, I no longer know—and handed them to *Maman*.

"Here," *Maman* said to Armand. "Keep the beans in your mouth to soften while I clean the wound."

In a few minutes, she split the beans and applied them to the gash. It required five halves to cover the wound.

"Do not remove them until they fall off. Then you will have very little scarring."

Well, no more swimming that day.

But everyone got acquainted with Armand Bald from Biddeford, Maine, on that truly special afternoon at Wells Beach.

Deep romance bloomed for Laurette and Armand—they celebrated their Fiftieth Wedding Anniversary in October, 1992, a long and beautiful half century for them.

CHAPTER 13

▼

For a few years, I sometimes felt too grown-up for Adrienne and Louise, and yet too young for my seven older sisters. And not much interested in the pastimes of Paul and Henri—except for the ballroom dancing.

Dancing had become a joy for all the Tétreau siblings. And Henri was my teacher. But I believe dancing came naturally to all of us, the same as singing. And in the same way the movies from the Golden Age of Hollywood enchanted all of us.

On many Saturday and Sunday matinees, I slipped out with Adrienne and stood in line early at the Capitol Theater to buy tickets for our big sisters' boy friends. Our reward for standing in the ticket line was our own ten-cent ticket to see the same movie.

I loved those movies. And the movie stars. Loretta Young and Ingrid Bergman were my favorites. And because we had aways been a singing family, Bing Crosby was also a special idol.

"Oh, *Maman*, you should see Loretta Young's beautiful gowns," Delia often said. Or Rose. Or Laurette. And off they'd go to the movies again, with *Maman,* to get fashion ideas. *Maman* could copy any dress her daughters wanted. I doubt any young girl's wardrobe in the whole U.S.A. looked as much like Loretta Young's as ours did.

Although the Tétreau family loved to sing and go to the movies, dancing with the boys eventually won out as everyone's favorite pastime.

Adrienne and I rarely went anywhere without the other. And when she was old enough, we were allowed to attend the church dances on Saturday evenings, as long as we returned home together.

Maman always waited up for us when we came home from any outing—and continued the habit even after we really had grown up.

"Faut-il rester toujours jusqu'à la fin serrer la porte, importe où?" she asked. Do you always have to stay to the very end, to lock up the place, wherever you go?"

But secretly, we knew *Maman* was pleased her girls were popular and happy.

✳   ✳   ✳   ✳

After the eighth grade, Paul and Henri went to the Sanford High School, pleased to be with the older students, but girls at St. Ignatius Catholic school just changed classrooms and teachers. No boys after the eighth grade. No sports, no music lessons, no special school dances.

Now I knew the Sanford High School had a Sweetheart Dance coming up soon and I really wanted to be at that one. So I called my friend, Irene, who attended the high school.

"Irene, it's Claire. Will you do me a favor?"

"Sure, Claire."

Little easy-going Claire suddenly turned brazen. "Tell Lionel La Flamme that Claire wants him to take her to that Sweetheart Dance."

My heart flip-flopped as I spoke. And continued in the same manner until the following afternoon, when Irene called back. I took a few deep breaths. Well, what was done, was done.

I could tell Irene was surprised, because Lionel La Flamme was in fact Mr. Football and Irene couldn't believe he could be so excited about going to the special dance with Claire Tétreau from St. Ignatius.

But he was.

Mr. Football was a great dancer and the evening was a success, but as usual I moved on to the next dance and a new boy named Gerard, who knew many fancy steps and led them easily. What fun we had.

The whirl continued. Carl Fenderson's Senior Prom. Carl was very proud of his graduation picture and was quick to show me. I thought he looked quite handsome, too, and waited for him to give me a copy. I truly wanted one but of course I couldn't ask and simply waited for him to offer one. But he didn't. That put a damper on the dance and was, in fact, the end of Carl Fenderson. I sometimes wondered how I could be so forward one moment and unbelievably timid the next.

But Adrienne spoke. "You always do that," she said.

"Do what?" I asked.

"Well, you go to a dance with someone and like him a lot, and then you think about silly things and move on to someone else."

I knew what Adrienne meant. And she was right. I always found a reason to move on. The story of my life.

"Carl Fenderson isn't Catholic. Or French, either." I spoke softly, with no vigor in my protest.

I'm not sure now what I was afraid of, but how many of us truly have tip-top, A-one, smooth-working brains at the age of sixteen?

None of the Tétreau sisters had problems finding boy friends. With ten sisters in one household, boys flocked around us.

More than once, they dropped by to see me when I had already gone to the movies with someone else.

But the dances—oh, the dances.

Old Orchard Beach pier and Wells Beach Ballroom were the gathering places for dancers in the summer.

Every year, the Elks Lodge had three formal affairs, always elegant, always exciting. And *Maman* said, *"C'est le temps de se faire belle."* Time to spruce up.

And she fashioned pretty Loretta Young style dresses for us with help from Rose and Delia. Rose and Delia seemed always to be the two *Maman* depended on the most.

And the afternoon before the Elks' Annual Winter Ball, a gorgeous sunny day after a winter wonderland snow storm, the sisters went to see Antoinette in the doctors' office for a few minutes under the ultra violet light.

Voilà! Summer suntan at the Christmas Ball.

But how to pin a gardenia corsage on a strapless gown?

"You can wrap it around your wrist, Claire," Laurette said.

"I don't want it on my wrist," I said. I might have sounded a bit petulant. Actually, I was excited in the manner of my

Number Ten status at long last being able to mingle with my big sisters at the Elks' Ball.

"Tie the corsage around your neck," Henri joked, as he stuck his head in the door. Because Henri was my dancing instructor, I was always grateful to him and laughed at his jokes, funny or not.

"What about tape?" I asked. "I know we have white medical tape around here someplace."

So my search began—in drawers and cabinets, on shelves— until I found the tape and practiced with it until the white tape and the white gardenia became as one.

Laurette still tied her corsage on her wrist, but I was the object of many stares and questions that night with a gardenia corsage taped so delicately on a bare shoulder no one could tell how it was managed.

The gardenia aroma permeated and tantalized everyone. Especially me. To this day gardenias are my favorite flower and the scent always sends me back to my first Elks' Ball.

Sometimes, Adrienne and I had the pick of what to wear to a dance after the older sisters had left with their dates.

Rose had the best choices, always very chic. I still remember her sheath dress with one side white and the other side black.

One night, after the big girls left, I chose to wear Rose's black and white sheath. Really daring of me.

The next day, a friend of Rose's said to her, "Claire certainly wore a fetching dress at the dance last night."

"Oh?" Rose asked. "What color was that dress?"

"Black and white," the friend replied. "Half and half. Your beautiful sheath, actually. And Claire topped it all off with socks and saddle shoes."

Rose laughed. "She loves those saddle shoes."

Well, I heard about this conversation later. And dear Rose never even scolded me.

               ✳   ✳   ✳   ✳

Henri had taught me very well how to dance. My dance books were always full. And my two big brothers who often went to the same dances kept my dance partners honorable—with a shove here and a push there, as might be required.

Well then, so no Tétreau sister was ever a wallflower.

Our home was always the meeting place for our friends although *Maman* did not want us to have only one special pal.

"She just wants us home, safe. And for herself," Adrienne explained.

Adrienne could always explain anything I needed to know.

CHAPTER 14

▼

Sometimes my mind slipped back to our early days on State Street when Papa was alive and busy with his Tailor Shop and Dry Cleaning business. Such a long time ago. What would he think now of our three-story mansion on Church Street? And how could he ever believe our fun-loving Vickie had become our breadwinner?

Because for some time, Vickie's Beauty Salon had truly been our main source of income.

I forgot Papa for the moment and thought about Vickie. And how secretly, just now and then, I wished I could be more like her. Well, just in some ways. I frowned. Well, not really. Vickie was Vickie and Claire was Claire. And that was good enough for me. Most of the time.

So Vickie was a prize-winning hair stylist, an expert in her work.

But she was not a business woman.

And it was not surprising she received an official letter from the Internal Revenue Service with an order to meet with their agent.

So with her usual aplomb, Vickie settled down with the agent to chat.

"Well, let's see your books," the agent began, his voice placid, his manner calm, his face enigmatic.

When Vickie didn't answer, he asked again in the same way. "Where are your books?"

"What books?" replied Vickie at last, her eyes wide and her mouth still slightly open to help her breathe.

Vickie had no books. No bookkeeping of any kind. I suppose in some ways that could sound ideal. But of course, it wasn't. Everyone in the family dropped the money as it was earned in a drawer and helped themselves from the same drawer whenever money was needed.

Naturally, because of this lack of financial management, I never had any money of my own. I often wished I were working at the mills and collecting a paycheck.

But what was more important, the IRS investigator stuck around.

He watched our place for six months.

A fact. For six months he parked his car across the street. And watched. And watched. And sometimes he pushed his glasses back up on his nose and ran his hand across his graying hair, and ambled over to the house to talk to *Maman*.

At the end of six months he spoke again to Vickie.

"Your clients traipse in and out all day. All female. Six months ago I even asked your mother what was going on in there."

"I know."

"I gathered—from her French—I don't really speak French—" he paused and Vickie inhaled a long thin breath as she waited for him to continue.

"Your mother said you owned a beauty salon. And the whole bunch of you were hairdressers."

"That is exactly right."

"But you have no financial records."

"True."

"So actually I'm no wiser than I was six months ago when I decided she ran a school for girls."

"Well, I think you know us better now." Vickie had recovered some of her sense of well-being, and glanced at the agent with a bit more of her usual verve.

"Of course. Your mother, Aurelie, is a wonderful person. Trustworthy and honest. I know there's no fraud going on here."

"Thank you."

"But you should try to learn about writing down a few important financial figures from time to time. In an accounting ledger."

Vickie glanced up and smiled ever so faintly. "Maybe one of my sisters might try to learn how to do that."

"Well, it would be a start." The IRS agent sighed deeply, then looked straight into Vickie's eyes. "You really must make the effort. You must."

Vickie squirmed just a tiny bit. "Are we okay then? For now?" she asked. "If we—you know, if we learn some things."

He nodded slowly and heaved in a gulp of air that for a moment straightened his drooping shoulders. He apparently knew fraud and trickery were not involved.

"I see no evidence of deceit or cheating, no intentional deception," he said.

But I think he also had known from the first moment he'd talked to Vickie, nothing was ever going to change her habits. He sensed something resolute in her. She knew exactly who she was. And liked what she knew. No sense in changing what was perfectly all right the way it was.

So the agent smiled and said, "Everything is okay now, but—" he stopped and began again, "but if you ever get another letter from the IRS, please ask for me. I don't want anyone else to be subjected to this."

He handed Vickie his business card, stood up and dismissed her.

But no question. Books or no books, Vickie's Beauty Salon was a success.

And years later, in 1979, at age sixty-five, Vickie was called back to the Hairdressers' National Convention in New York, to be honored as the oldest living recipient of the International Grand Prize for Haircutting and Styling.

Some evenings the girls worked late. Other nights they invited friends over to play cards. Whatever the mood. But something noisy and happy was always going on in our big house.

When a space opened in the doctors' large office building, Rose, a creative hairdresser herself, decided to try managing a beauty shop of her own. With *Maman's* backing, of course. Rose said she would keep books properly. And she did. Rose had a definite flair and was well-liked by her customers. Paul and Laurette helped as needed. And so did I.

But when Rose married Edgar Des Rosiers early in 1940, *Maman* gave the salon to Paul.

I always thought Rose Des Rosiers was an interesting name for my dear sister. She was a lovely bride. And Edgar was so suave. At the auspicious occasion of their wedding Mass, I was in the choir and sang Schubert's Ave Maria solo. Rose and Edgar looked up at me during the recessional and smiled their thank you. Later, Edgar said he'd never heard that Ave Maria sung more beautifully. Of course, I believed him.

I was so proud and happy, but at the same time, I wondered how we could possibly manage without Rose. My wonderful family had already begun its insidious self-destruction. Rose was not the first—

Antoinette was married.

Bertha was married.

Delia was married.

But it was Rose's marriage that shattered me. Made me realize our wonderful family was disintegrating one wedding at a time. Of course, new in-laws were added and babies would come and our Twelve would soar to a greater number. But of course, everybody knows that isn't the same.

I also knew deep in my heart—as long as *Maman* was with us we would always be a special family.

Maman would see to that.

CHAPTER 15

───────▼───────

I believe almost everyone finds the teen years full of surprises and excitement, a time of learning, a kaleidoscope of fresh new feelings, not always understandable.

One would think with seven older sisters I might have learned a thing or two from them by osmosis, but I guess life doesn't always work that way. Each sister had to manage her own learning processes, experience her emotions personally. I, myself, took a long time with it all.

Anyway, my sisters were all different. No one was like Vickie. Only Marguerite chose a cloistered life. As close pals as Adrienne and I were, our personalities were unique. We were compatible because she was serious and I was the vivacious, amicable follower.

However, like my sisters, I did survive a few teenage crushes. But unlike my sisters, none of my puppy loves burgeoned with substance and depth. None flourished into love and marriage, but all eventually passed into nothingness, and unfortunately left me none the wiser.

Cousin Eddie was my first. He lived in Holyoke, Massachusetts, with my Uncle Thomas Langlois and his family. So Eddie and I were a long-distance twosome and only together when relatives visited.

When we went to Holyoke, Eddie was very attentive. One time he invited me to attend Sunday Mass with him. How exciting. I wore a robin's egg blue A-line dress *Maman* had made for me directly from a photo in a fashion magazine. And a large picture hat of the same color over my long, dark hair. I thought I was quite smashing. And so did Eddie.

After Mass, as we strolled down the tree-lined avenue, Eddie turned to me. His dark eyes sparkled and his voice quivered slightly through his bravado.

"Have you ever been kissed?" he asked. Just like that. No warning. No casual lead-in to the embarrassing question.

I froze for a moment and couldn't answer at all.

"Well?" Eddie prompted.

I hated to say 'no', but 'no' was the truth. And I told him the truth.

So he kissed me.

Right there, after Mass, in broad daylight, under the trees.

Well, as long as the truth is foremost here, that first kiss wasn't much of a kiss. I'd seen enough romantic movies to realize that. Eddie didn't know any more than I did. Even in my inexperienced state, I was pretty sure he, himself would have to do better.

Cousin Eddie and I corresponded for years, little love notes under the stamps, but we lived too far apart and never actually dated. First cousins—well, that was a definite taboo, anyway.

But I certainly had a crush on Cousin Eddie.

*   *   *   *

Now George Hawes, Junior, was another heart throb who didn't live in Sanford.

We met on a two-week vacation Laurette, Adrienne, and I took together in Tent City at Alton Bay.

"What a wonderful place to relax," Adrienne said, as she admired the lush green forest that encircled the tents.

Three meals a day were served family-style in a large dining room. On our first Sunday dinner the manager of Tent City announced a surprise.

"A brand new product is on the market that we are serving for your dessert tonight," he said. "Called Toll House Cookies."

Well, those cookies were certainly a treat and they are still my favorites.

But the best treat of our entire vacation was meeting George Hawes, Junior, from Medford, Massachusetts.

George—we called him Junior—was a college student, short, stocky, with light brown hair, and he wore horned-rimmed glasses. Best of all, he was a wonderful dancer. What else does any girl need?

In the evenings, the Tent City dining room was transformed into a dance hall, which was where we first met Junior.

So Laurette, Adrienne and I changed for the evening from our daytime playsuits to our dresses, ankle socks and saddle oxfords.

"This dancing is not formal," a group of teenage girls advised us as we emerged from our tent. They stood outside, barefooted and in shorts.

The second evening we dressed up as usual for dancing and the same group wore thongs with their shorts.

The third evening they wore clean shorts and regular shoes.

And then for the rest of the week, out came the Sunday dresses, socks and fancy shoes.

Even the boys combed their hair.

"You see what we did?" Laurette asked Adrienne and me. "And we never once opened our mouths."

Adrienne and I stared at Laurette. What she said was true. And an unexpected surge of power I'd never felt before flooded through me. I was actually awed by that experience of our tacit influence.

And I believe Junior also realized what had transpired.

My friendship with Junior began on the Tent City dance floor and extended beyond our vacation at Alton Bay.

Many times he drove from Medford, Massachusetts to Sanford, Maine, to see me.

Once, he said, "Claire, will you go to my school prom with me?"

I was so excited I couldn't speak.

"You'll stay at our home in Medford for the weekend."

I remained mute.

"You'll be quite safe, you know, with my mother and sisters there."

Of course, I accepted. And the next day I took *Maman* to see a Loretta Young movie, luckily in town, to get the pattern of the lovely flowing dress she wore in one dance scene. And I ended up with a gorgeous white chiffon off-the-shoulder formal gown to wear to Junior's prom. But he was the handsome one—in his tuxedo. I'd never seen anyone in a tuxedo before. When I saw Junior, I could barely breathe.

And in the height of the general, overall, ecstasy of the prom, a local girl said to me, "You look like a beautiful cameo." What a terrific compliment for some one from small town Sanford, Maine. All thanks to the special dress *Maman* made. I floated on air for the rest of the night.

I spent prom weekends with Junior's family and he spent many nights on our living room sofa, when he drove to Sanford to see me.

I told Junior I wanted—one day—a big home like on a southern plantation, with the white columns across the front.

"If that's what you want, I'll get it for you," Junior said. And the tone of his voice told me he meant what he said. I smiled and often thought about my big home with the white columns.

But it never happened.

The last time he was in Sanford, some of us piled in his car and some in the Olds and we spent the day at Long Pond, our favorite, in the nearby town of Shapleigh.

As soon as we arrived, Paul and Henri ran across the road to dive off the bridge. The swan dive was their favorite.

The day was spent in much revelry, hours in the water with many swan dives, later a bonfire with hot dogs and hamburgers, and toasted marshmallows.

As darkness overtook the sunlight, we returned home, tired but happy, from our Sunday outing at Long Pond in Shapleigh.

As usual, Junior was offered the living room sofa for the night.

Junior and I were friends for many years. He was always so very comfortable to be with.

After he graduated from college, he went to work designing war machinery equipment. In a catastrophic ammunition explosion in the plant, he suffered burns over his entire body. For six months, he was treated inside a bunting filled with ice and for another year he spent hours and hours in therapy and treatments.

I never saw him after our day at Long Pond in Shapleigh.

"I don't want you to visit me the way I look now," he wrote.

We exchanged many letters, but slowly his mail stopped coming.

One still, cold, bitter winter morning, *Maman* reminded me Junior was neither Catholic nor French.

She just wanted me to feel better, ease my pain. I know that.
But it didn't help.

CHAPTER 16

▼

The financial depression that had paralyzed the country since 1929 never really released its hold until Imperial Japan bombed Pearl Harbor, Oahu, Hawaii, U.S.A. Then everything simply slipped into World War II with a new kind of fear and deprivation to grip the people.

"A date which will live in infamy," President Roosevelt said of December 7, 1941."

Laurette, thousands of miles away, was the one who screamed first in our house, as the news spread by radio through Sanford, Maine, and all the cities and towns and hamlets in the country.

"Armand is there!" Laurette shrieked. "He's there, in Pearl Harbor, on his ship."

She ran through the house, frantic, and we stared after her, helpless.

"*Qu'est-ce qui se passe là-bas?*" *Maman* asked, her voice anxious. What's happening over there?

We took turns explaining how Japanese planes destroyed half the U.S. Navy in a surprise attack as sailors, unaware, strolled the decks of their moored ships on that early, misty Sunday morning in Hawaii.

But the miracle of Armand Bald was his weekend pass. He had joined the navy a few months earlier because he could not find a job in the sluggish economy. But, thanks to his pass, he was not on his ship that fateful Sunday morning in Pearl Harbor.

Because telephone lines were clogged all day—no such thing as e-mail then—our news didn't come until late in the evening when Armand's telephone call reached Laurette.

After their chat was over, she fell on the living room sofa in blessed relief.

The following day, Monday, December 8, 1941, our brother, Paul, stood in a long line at the recruiting center. A week later, he was sworn in as a Marine, off to boot camp, and then on to war in the Pacific.

Soon Henri joined the Navy.

But the war news was dark and bleak. The days held no good reports in spite of solid national togetherness and purpose. The whole country, even the isolationists, joined with a single-minded determination to win the war.

For months the Japanese ground out victory after victory. Rationing of food, gasoline and many needed staples became a way of life in the U.S. Oleomargarine, commonly referred to as oleo, was introduced for butter. The white mass was kneaded and blended with yellow coloring before serving. But it didn't fool anyone. And no cars for civilian use were manufactured until the war ended.

Our Antoinette, whose husband and two brothers were away at war, was on our local rationing board. And being the honest person she was, she issued not one extra coupon to her kin—

nor anyone else. Like all of us, she did her best to help win the war and later she received an award for the greatest sale of government bonds in the state of Maine.

By 1942, the plush looms at the Goodall Mills had been converted to war production. Most of them wove canvas duck, some made alpaca linings for aviator jackets and other fabrics for the armed forces.

Being at war was everyone's new life. No one knew when the war would end, but everyone knew we would win it.

*   *   *   *

Civilians as well as military wanted to do their part for the war effort. We were all in it together.

One of my tasks was to write to the local soldiers, to give them a few encouraging words from home.

"Do you have your list?" *Maman* asked. "Do you know who you're writing to?"

"Yes, here," I said and waved the list at her. "Quite a few— I'm not sure if—" My voice trailed off. After all, Antoinette was the true letter-writer of the family. Now me.

"No typewriter," Adrienne said.

I shook my head. I knew my letters would be hand-written. But my brilliant solution was carbon paper, five or six deep. I knew the soldiers and sailors were happy to get news from home, no matter how it came.

And the letters of thanks were V-mail with many of the forbidden words cut out by the censor before mailing.

From one soldier I received an answer that woke me up sharply.

"I don't mind if you call me Frank when my name is Daniel," he wrote. "I don't mind if I have to read the letter in a mirror because you had one carbon on the wrong side. I don't mind if the letter is blurred. But please don't send me another empty envelope."

I took special care after that.

*   *   *   *

But life at home didn't stop.

Three Tétreau sisters including me were in Boston, Massachusetts, for refresher courses in hairdressing, and one morning, we visited the Lunden Turkish Bath to relax.

A sauna bath occupant was pleasant and friendly and asked our names.

"We are Laurette, Claire, and Adrienne Tétreau, from Sanford, Maine," Adrienne replied.

The lady's face brightened. "Oh, well, my goodness," she said, "could Joseph Paul Tétreau, the great war hero so prominent in the news now, possibly be your brother?"

We smiled and nodded in unison.

"Well, the country is so proud of him! I am Rose Kennedy and I must add my felicitations to your family."

That was a delightful accolade from the great lady.

Paul received a thank-you letter from President Truman. In a ceremony in Boston, Paul was awarded the Bronze Star and two Purple Hearts.

Paul was a veteran of bombing raids, naval shelling, bayonet attacks and the full flood of the Pacific War.

After boot camp he was sent to Guadalcanal, on to New Britain and the bloody battles of Palaus and Paleliu.

The family was proud of our Corporal Joseph Paul Tétreau, who commanded his fellow Marines because he was the highest ranking Marine still alive when their Division was pinned down in an open field by enemy machine gun fire from nearby caves. He led all the American lives to safety that day.

His Marine buddies kidded him for having ten sisters and being a part of a family hairdressing business.

"Why don't they all become Permanent Waves?" they laughed.

But when the war was over and at Paul's own wedding reception, the bride's brother, a priest, said to his sister, "So this is your hairdresser!" And later he admitted he was thankful for his white collar after glancing at Paul's forbidding expression.

✳   ✳   ✳   ✳

While the war was still going on, and *Maman* waited for her boys to come home she decided to turn our huge barn, with the hayloft on the top, into apartments.

She and the older girls went to the bank to borrow money and in time the barn was slowly transformed. A good plan to keep *Maman's* mind occupied.

But she was unable to complete her project.

On Tuesday of Easter week, 1945, *Maman* had a massive stroke. And another one on Wednesday that completely paralyzed her. And then she was gone.

The shock to the family was awful.

Paul had just returned from his grueling war experiences and a long stint in the hospital for malaria, battle fatigue and wounds.

Henri and his wife came from California.

Both Paul and Henri believed, with terrible guilt, their arrival caused *Maman's* death, but the doctor assured them she simply waited for them and would have waited longer if they had not come then.

We were all home for her service several months before the war ended. Never was such a showing of love from all our relatives and friends. Forty-nine automobiles were filled with the citizenry of Sanford and neighboring towns who came to pay their respects. Stores and the city offices were closed for the morning in deference to our *Maman*.

But she was gone and her large, beautiful family crumbled. We didn't know how to behave without her. We had no leader, no understanding soul to comfort and guide. We were no longer a compatible unit, but twelve lost souls who didn't know how to cope.

Even I, the most easy-going of all the Tétreau siblings, sensed the change in the air. Without *Maman* here and in control, all sorts of personal attitudes and behavior surfaced that were never seen nor felt before.

Oh, *Maman*, what has happened to us?

Maman left no Will, which added to the confusion.

So Vickie remained in the family home—because her beauty salon was located there. Adrienne and I were given the 1941 Oldsmobile—what would we, and Louise, too, have done without wheels? And *Maman's* $10,000 insurance policy was divided among the others.

Undercurrents of discontent and disbelief whooshed around us and allowed stabs of anger and hurt to surface momentarily, before a quick retreat.

I was devastated that our lovely family was so shattered about everything. I would have agreed to anything.

Adrienne, Louise and I were the only unmarried girls and went to live with Rose and Edgar in Biddeford and worked for them in their beauty salon.

*   *   *   *

August was always two-week vacation time for us. In 1945, we still had not recovered from *Maman's* death and Adrienne, Louise and I went to Camp Ohivo, a summer place at a lake in the mountains. Vacations were always near a lake, an ocean or a river.

That first evening, we were in a canoe and watched the falling stars in the clear night sky with its million stars. Maybe *Maman* was—

But the next evening, the entire sky was ablaze with falling stars. We were in awe.

"It's a meteor shower," a stranger explained, and added, "Such a shower occurs once in forty years. We're lucky to be here."

Oh, yes, we were lucky to have witnessed such a spectacle. But the experience was deeper than that. Spiritual. As if God shared his sparkling stars with us. Almost as if *Maman* were there with us. And Him. We were still mellow with it when our vacation ended.

As we drove home through Portland, the entire city bustled and screamed. A day of jubilant celebration. VE Day! The long awaited end to the war in Europe. We were elated, too. First a celestial phenomenon in the sky and then the victory in Europe.

But we didn't join the hysterical revelers. We drove to the park and gave our thanks quietly.

Then we drove home.

∗   ∗   ∗   ∗

Adrienne and I had planned a double wedding for February, 1946. But at the last minute I couldn't go through with this added change in my life. I became Adrienne's bridesmaid, instead, and Louise and I remained with Rose and Edgar for one more year.

Then I had the double wedding with Louise. She and Rose took care of the details, all very elegant. I thought someone might suspect my lack of enthusiasm and prevent a mistake, but no one did. Instead all was lovely, exactly as planned for the big day.

But my heart wasn't in it.

And in a few weeks, dear Rose and Edgar left for California—which was the end of the world for me.

CHAPTER 17

▼

I thought *Maman* would always be with us, at least live to be very old. Not abandon us at age fifty-nine. She was always so busy. So loved. So loving.

Now, without her, the road ahead seemed endless and forbidding. Lonely.

But no going back.

Childhood had already closed its doors.

In time, the twelve of us married—well, not Marguerite. And our number began to multiply with new spouses and children, uncles and aunts, and eventually, our large tribe was scattered from Maine to California.

But insidiously, the beloved siblings I cherished and needed so desperately—my security blanket—diminished. Unobtrusively, as the new generation appeared, the old originals faltered and slipped away, even if it were to a desert playground in Southern California, or the Mount Merici Convent in Waterville, Maine. Worse for me, if it were to a higher glory.

Actually, with *Maman* gone, we twelve, as if afloat on the winds, no longer existed as a loving, special unit. Or perhaps everything was just carefully gift-wrapped and placed tenderly in the bottom drawer of memory.

Anyway, my story truly ends here.

*   *   *   *

But life continued.

My dream world, where I worried about nothing, slowly metamorphosed into unadorned, unexpected, unyielding reality.

The essence of the early days will be with me always, but my existence became plain, predictable, mundane, even though change is what the world is made of.

For a few seconds back then, after *Maman* died, my mind drifted to our Bébé Louise. She never knew our papa. Didn't sit on his lap while he ate his dinner. Or peer into his soft, dark, happy eyes. Not even once. How really sad. And Louise was just seventeen when *Maman* died.

I wanted to put my arms around my baby sister, comfort her. She'd missed so much—but I can't recall now whether I actually did that. The family spirit was to look out for one another. Did I look out for Louise when *Maman* left us?

I don't remember.

But finally, in 1984, after all the years of separation and busy adulthood and motherhood, *la pièce de résistance* fell from heaven: a Reunion. For seven of us—yes, we are now down to seven—Antoinette, Rose, Laurette, Marguerite, Adrienne, Louise and me. Ages from fifty-seven to seventy-six. At Rose's home in La Quinta, California, where she and Edgar lived on Calle Serenas, which became a crowded street for our joyous greeting with many neighbors present to meet Rose's sisters.

Four flew in from the East and Antoinette and I from San Diego.

Rose and Edgar, always the perfect host and hostess, were ready for us. A glass of wine, fingertip asparagus sticks in butter dip, mini sandwiches, to refresh.

Cots were borrowed from the neighbors to bed down the crowd if any one could relinquish togetherness for sleep. Most of the time non-stop chatter prevailed.

"You should have seen us on the plane," Adrienne said when she had everyone's attention. "The couple behind us asked if we were sisters. Oh yes, I said and the two sitting in front of us are also our sisters. Laurette and Marguerite turned around and smiled. Then I said that's not all. Three more are waiting breathlessly in California for our arrival.

"By that time everyone nearby on the plane was interested in our conversation."

"So what else did you tell them?" Rose asked Adrienne.

"Well, I said we were having a reunion with sisters we hadn't seen in ages. We were all enjoying ourselves by that time and we laughed and began a conversation that lasted the entire trip."

In La Quinta, we started an on-going conversation that didn't stop for five days, interrupted only by dinners, sightseeing tours or sleep. Otherwise non-stop reminiscing.

"Remember when—" someone would prompt and the memories flooded through all of us.

Remember when—

Our dinner that first night in La Quinta had been carefully planned, totally gourmet with Maine lobster, naturally, and vegetable soup from *Maman's* recipe, skinny asparagus, squash and zucchini. As usual, Rose and Edgar managed to bring elegance into the already euphoric atmosphere.

"Remember when *Maman* bought the two baby chicks for Easter?" Adrienne asked at Rose's beautifully appointed dinner table.

We all remembered. *Maman* often bought chicks.

"And one was done in by Tallulah, the cat," Laurette said, a little twist of a smile at the corners of her mouth.

And we all recalled the verbal thrashing Tallulah received from the whole family, especially *Maman*, Tallulah's main love.

From then on the remaining chick was protected. Not one feather was touched by the neighborhood predators.

This proud cock became the morning alarm clock for the nearby world and he followed *Maman* around like a puppy.

And being so close to St. Ignatius, the rooster actually followed *Maman* one Sunday all the way down the center aisle of the church.

Chuckles filtered through the parishioners as another Tétreau antic amused them.

And Paul was late for Mass after running the rooster home.

"Speaking of *Maman's* rooster being in the wrong place, remember when that old man stumbled up the stairs in our house by mistake in the middle of the night?" Laurette asked.

"What old man?" from Antoinette.

"The poor soul who had too much to drink and went home to his rooming house, which just happened to be our new home on Church Street. We all waved our arms and screeched at him and chased him back down the stairs. We scared the daylights out of him and probably the neighborhood, too."

"How do you know he thought it was his old rooming house?" Marguerite asked quietly.

"Because it had been a rooming house before the doctor owned it," Laurette answered and we were all still for a moment as our minds slipped back to the old man who 'came home.'

During those seconds of thoughtfulness, I realized Marguerite, for all her sixty-seven years, still had the aura of youth and the innocence of a teenager who had never in any way been touched by the reality of life. My heartbeat quickened, as I gazed at her and deep down I wondered what she might be thinking at that moment.

✳   ✳   ✳   ✳

We spent hours in Rose's swimming pool, more than once took the boat trip around the lake, or strolled around it.

We picked our own juicy red breakfast grapefruit from a tree in their garden.

But the biggest surprise, shock really, was the effect seven look-alike svelte older sisters had on the diners in the restaurant when we went out to dinner one night.

Rose and Edgar entered first, then one by one we filed by the tables. The patrons were surprised to see seven, graceful, look-alike copies, all with the same chiseled profile of our dear French *Maman*.

Heads spun around, one double-take at a time. We were truly stunned to realize the excitement we had caused, as if we were slightly aging septuplets worth taking a few extra glimpses of.

I guess you can take the girl from the family, but you can't take the family from the girl, especially seven of them.

And then we'd reached our table and soon were back again to Remember when—this time from Louise.

And as if we were still remembering the old inebriated man who had forgotten where he lived, she began, "Speaking of strangers in the house, do you remember when that young man came to the door and asked for work in exchange for dinner?"

"Oh, yes," I said and the others nodded.

And I thought back to that knock at our side door, and our generous *Maman* who invited the young man in.

When he spotted our piano in the den, all thoughts of work and food disappeared and he quietly asked. "May I play a song on the piano?"

But *Maman,* in broken English, said, "Food first, then music."

My name is Jon," he said.

And we all introduced ourselves.

After dinner, Jon headed straight for the piano. He caressed the top of the keyboard lovingly before he sat down. Soon, by heart, his concert music filled the room. The whole family listened. We sat everywhere, close to the piano as well as on the stairs. Jon played through the evening hours without stopping. Chopin, Mozart, Liszt.

Finally, long after our bedtime, *Maman* insisted Jon stay and sleep on the couch.

Next morning, we chatted with him before he left us forever.

"Every time I come close to a piano or organ, I just have to play," he said with a smile.

"It was beautiful," Louise said.

"The louder the better," Jon said. "I go into many churches in the late evenings," he continued. "Sometimes, I wake up the pastors who wonder where the music is coming from."

Jon said he could never get employment at a church because his playing was too loud.

"Well, why didn't he soften it up, if he wanted a job," Antoinette asked us many years later in La Quinta.

"Because he wanted to play the way he wanted to play," Louise said. "I understand that."

I glanced at Louise and wondered whether she always wanted to sing the way she wanted to sing, but—

"The last I heard about Jon was he had a job washing dishes," Louise added. "Imagine his washing dishes when he could play the piano so magnificently."

And I thought for just a quick moment maybe our little Louise was thinking about her own never-achieved operatic possibilities.

I studied her a long time from across the room and wondered whether she actually was talking about herself.

"Sing us a song, Louise," I said impulsively, but my voice was a bit choked up and nobody heard me through the cacophony of our chatter.

"If Jon forcefully altered the direction his life really needed to follow," Louise said, "he will forever lack the grace he needs so desperately."

I thought a long time about Louise's words but I never really understood them. I wasn't sure what she meant by grace.

But I think it might have meant a gift from God shouldn't be mishandled.

Antoinette Laurette Marguerite Adrienne Claire Louise Rose

EPILOGUE

━━━━━━━━━━━━━━━ ▼ ━━━━━━━━━━━━━━━

We could never finish all the Remember whens—the lost jade ring Papa gave Antoinette as the firstborn. The spilled Shalimar, thanks to me, that scented the neighborhood. When Henri and his friend fell from the hayloft. How I learned to like my one syllable name. When Paul and Henri played with too many matches. Making caramel taffy with snow. And so on. And on. And on.

But we had only five days in La Quinta—not enough time for all the Remember whens.

So my story truly ended after La Quinta—except for this important *dénouement*:

When my marriage to the father of my five children ended, I became a single mom.

And a real estate agent.

I was successful because I got along well with all kinds of people. Paperwork was not my favorite aspect of the job, but my boss didn't mind helping me since I brought in enough sales to become a member of the Million Dollar Club.

Even so, life was a truly lonely time for me.

Dancing was my most enjoyable pastime. I was the only single member of a Smooth Dancing group that met bi-monthly. We dressed formally, long gown, black tie.

Nell Dickenson, the president of the group, called me early one morning and got right to the point.

"Good morning, Claire. The Harvest Moon Ball at the Hotel del Coronado is on Saturday night. I have an escort for you. You'll love him. I know he's the man for you."

I was speechless.

Nell pushed me hard as she was aware I avoided even a minor commitment.

But I did love to dance and the Hotel del was a lovely place and Nell would never give up, anyway.

My blind date, Mr. Stewart Brandt, who had recently lost his wife, was experiencing the same push.

However, Nell won out.

On that special night we met at Nell's apartment. I arrived in an ice-blue and white formal gown, and a dab or two of Shalimar, and Mr. B wore a light blue tuxedo and drove us in a white Lincoln Continental.

Even if I'd been called Cinderella, I would not have believed that evening.

The Hotel del was in full splendor; the orchestra played our kind of music; Mr. B and I moved together—actually we glided together—as one. After a few dances, Mr. B. smiled and said, "Move over, Fred."

I knew he was referring to Fred Astaire.

That night was the beginning of a beautiful romance. Nell continued to push things along at a rapid pace.

Mr. B and I were married on Valentine's Day, 1985, and now in 2006 we've enjoyed twenty one years of dancing, of travel, of golf and boats, of entertaining, of watching sunsets over the Pacific Ocean, of serenity and contentment in our La Jolla mountain top home.

Often when we watched the sunsets together, I sent a little message to *Maman* with my head tilted upward and my eyes closed, "It's okay, *Maman*. Mr. B is neither Catholic nor French. But it's okay. He's from Massachusetts and likes crab cakes and clam chowder. He's a good man, right for me. We are happy.

But I am aware *Maman* knows all that and is pleased for us.

And Maman, I've become a poet in my old age, and this is what I wrote to Mr. B on Valentine's Day:

TO MY MR.B

Another anniversary, my pet.
   Valentine's Day, two thousand six.
How quickly time disappeared when I became your wife,
   And yet,
New memories and new meanings refilled our way of life.
   And now we're structured, quiet, peaceful, but
      Those exotic trips
      The formal dances
      The parties when you were the chef
Slip back to us, reborn, full blown.
   So on our Day of Hearts and Flowers
You say, "I sure love you."
   I smile and answer, "I sure love you, too."

Mrs. B

978-0-595-40958-7
0-595-40958-X